The Imitation of Christ

Selected Books in the
SkyLight Illuminations Series

The Imitation of Christ

Selections Annotated & Explained

Thomas à Kempis

Annotation by Paul Wesley Chilcote, PhD

Adapted from John Wesley's
The Christian's Pattern

Walking Together, Finding the Way ®
SKYLIGHT PATHS®
PUBLISHING
Woodstock, Vermont

The Imitation of Christ:
Selections Annotated & Explained

2012 Quality Paperback Edition, First Printing
Introductory materials, annotations, and back matter © 2012 by Paul Wesley Chilcote

All biblical quotations used in this work are from the New Revised Standard Version (NRSV) of the Bible.

Library of Congress Cataloging-in-Publication Data

Imitatio Christi. English. Selections.
    The imitation of Christ : selections annotated & explained / Thomas à Kempis ; annotated by Paul Wesley Chilcote ; adapted from John Wesley's The Christian's pattern. — Quality pbk. ed.
        p. cm. — (SkyLight illuminations)
    "Walking together, finding the way."
    Includes bibliographical references and index.
    ISBN 978-1-59473-434-2 (pbk.)
    1. Meditations. 2. Imitatio Christi. I. Thomas, à Kempis, 1380-1471. II. Chilcote, Paul Wesley, 1954- III. Wesley, John, 1703-1791. IV. Title.
    BV4821.C45 2012
    242—dc23
                                    2012018004

10 9 8 7 6 5 4 3 2 1

Manufactured in the United States of America

SkyLight Paths Publishing is creating a place where people of different spiritual traditions come together for challenge and inspiration, a place where we can help each other understand the mystery that lies at the heart of our existence.

SkyLight Paths sees both believers and seekers as a community that increasingly transcends traditional boundaries of religion and denomination—people wanting to learn from each other, *walking together, finding the way.*

SkyLight Paths, "Walking Together, Finding the Way" and colophon are trademarks of LongHill Partners, Inc., registered in the U.S. Patent and Trademark Office.

Walking Together, Finding the Way®
Published by SkyLight Paths® Publishing
A Division of LongHill Partners, Inc.
Sunset Farm Offices, Route 4, P.O. Box 237
Woodstock, VT 05091
Tel: (802) 457-4000   Fax: (802) 457-4004
www.skylightpaths.com

For Alyssa

Contents ☐

BOOK III
The Comfort of the Heart

BOOK IV
The Sacrament of Holy Communion

Preface ☐

The Imitation of Christ is the most widely read Christian devotional book next to the Bible. It has influenced the lives of thousands of people both inside and outside the Christian community. First appearing in published form around 1471, and emerging out of a spiritual renewal movement of the late medieval world known as the *devotio moderna*, a Latin term meaning modern devotion, this classic has been translated into more than fifty languages and has appeared in as many as three thousand editions. John Wesley, the founder of Methodism—an eighteenth-century movement of spiritual renewal in the Church of England—considered this book to be of such great importance that he produced some 120 editions in four different forms. The excerpts in this present volume are based on his translation and abridgement of the work published in 1741. He carried a copy of his pocket edition of this version in his saddlebag for half a century, until his death.

So why a new volume about such a widely read book of Christian devotion? Despite the fact that so many editions of this work remain in print, there are surprisingly few modern English versions that make the text accessible to contemporary readers. Moreover, the vast majority of the editions include little if any commentary to help readers in their own quest for spiritual vitality. This is particularly true of the many online versions of *The Imitation of Christ* that are easily accessible, but in many ways impenetrable because of the archaic language. This SkyLight Illuminations volume on *The Imitation of Christ* seeks to remedy this situation. I have modernized Wesley's English translation and have used his abridgement of the original text as a guide. One of the wonderful features of the SkyLight Illuminations series is the facing-page commentary format that er ables readers to enter into a dialogue with the ideas, images, and vision of this classic guide to the spiritual life with greater ease. My hope is that th s introduction to *The Imitation of Christ* will warm your heart, challenge ycur mind, and inspire you to pursue your journey into the heart of God with greater intentionality and zeal.

I prepared much of the commentary for this volume during a Wesley Heritage Pilgrimage to England, where I stayed in the shadow of Salisbury Cathedral at Sarum College, in the cathedral close. I woke every morning to the peal of the bells calling the community to prayer. I'd like to think that this providential connection, with such a monumental reminder of the medieval church and world, influenced my own reflections. Certainly, in many ways I felt transported from time to time into a different context, a world that the author of *The Imitation of Christ* both knew intimately and sought to reform. The experience of daily Eucharist in the cathedral ur doubtedly enhanced my reflections on Book IV in particular, and gave me a deeper sense of the centrality of this meal in the Christian journey.

Despite the fact that a setting like Salisbury Cathedral and the late medieval context of *The Imitation of Christ* represent a world far removed from that of my day-to-day life, I am struck by the continuity as well. Have we changed all that much as human beings in the past six hundred years? The spiritual guidance provided to the contemporary God-seeker in this work remains fresh, dynamic, and vital. It focuses on a religion of the heart—a vital connection with God in our innermost being. It advocates the cultivation of virtues, like humility and purity of intention, not through mimicry of Jesus, but by inviting the spirit of Jesus to dwell richly in our lives. It emphasizes the need to translate that life of love into daily action. *The Imitation of Christ* has changed me in some way every time I have read it. Through this opportunity to engage the spiritual insights of this timeless classic on a more intimate level, God has transformed me anew, and that is my prayer for every reader.

Many people have assisted me in this journey. I first read *The Imitation of Christ* in its original form in conjunction with a directed study I did with Dr. McMurry Richey on "Devotional Influences on the Life of John Wesley" as a seminary student at Duke Divinity School years ago. I still have my notes from the conversations "Mack" and I shared. He was a wise man. The edition I read for that purpose was the copy of the book in my father's library. I consulted it on many occasions in the process of producing this new volume, and even touching its binding and leafing through its pages brought back wonderful memories of my father's spiritual depth. The theme of community pervades *The Imitation of Christ*, and I owe a great debt of gratitude to so many others who have made this book possible. From a family that has supported me and labored with me at the dinner table to make each word count, to the printers and binders who transformed words on pages into this volume in your hands (or onto your electronic reader), I offer my heartfelt thanks.

Several friends and colleagues made a special effort to read my manuscript in its entirety and offered many helpful suggestions, particularly in the commentary. My deep gratitude, therefore, to Dr. John R. Tyson, editor of *Invitation to Christian Spirituality* and a fellow Wesley scholar, for his incisive reflections on the commentary; to Sharon Rowland, a disciple of Dallas Willard and keen advocate of Renovaré, for her many helpful suggestions and her commitment to pray for this volume; and to Rick Hatton, one of my students at Ashland Theological Seminary, who has now helped me bring two volumes in the SkyLight Illuminations series to completion. While their particular marks on this book are not immediately visible, I have no doubt that their contributions will help bring readers closer to God.

I dedicate this edition of a timeless classic to my granddaughter, Alyssa, whose parents, Anna and Bobby, are already teaching her what it really means to imitate Christ.

Introduction ☐

The words of the well-known Negro spiritual express a timeless ideal: "Lord, I want to be like Jesus, in my heart." Ever since the birth of the Christian religion over two millennia ago, followers of Jesus have sought to imitate his life. Whether they understand this vision of the Christian way in a literal or figurative sense, disciples of Jesus in every age have viewed this pursuit as an essential part of their spiritual journey. As they have looked back over the history of Christianity, they identify saintly figures who have imitated Jesus to the fullest possible measure. Francis of Assisi, for instance, stands out as one who cultivated a life that conformed fully to the life of Jesus. Closer to our own time, Mother Teresa of Calcutta, perhaps, falls into this same unique category. No doubt you know someone who is irresistibly like Jesus.

One of the earliest hymns of the church, recorded by St. Paul in Philippians 2:5–11, provides a portrait of Jesus that many have sought to emulate:

> Let the same mind be in you that was in Christ Jesus, who, though he was in the form of God, did not regard equality with God as something to be exploited, but emptied himself, taking the form of a slave, being born in human likeness. And being found in human form, he humbled himself and became obedient to the point of death—even death on a cross. (5–8)

The qualities of obedience, humility, service, and self-emptying love create the texture of this portrait. Throughout Christian history, devout followers of Jesus have prayed intentionally and cooperated with God's grace in a quest to realize these lofty virtues in their lives—to measure up to the "full stature of Christ" (Ephesians 4:13). In the fourteenth century, a movement began to spread throughout the church in Europe. It emphasized anew the need to pattern life on the model of Jesus and one of its members produced one of the greatest Christian devotional classics of all time—*The Imitation of Christ.*

The Origins of *The Imitation of Christ*

The origins of *The Imitation of Christ* lie in three particular but interconnected elements: a new movement of Christian spirituality, a community of devout followers of Jesus, and a simple Augustinian monk with the gift of communication.

Devotio Moderna (The Modern Devotion)

During the fourteenth and fifteenth centuries, the foundations of the church-centered European world began to quake and shake. The confluence of multiple forces led to the collapse of this "Age of Faith" and paved the way, at the same time, for the emergence of a new world birthed in an age of renaissance and reformation. The labor pangs of this new social and religious order continued until the beginning of the sixteenth century, when figures like Martin Luther, Ulrich Zwingli, and Thomas Cranmer played midwife to this new reality. Changes in Christian spirituality exerted a major influence in all of these developments.

The term "Modern Devotion," in some ways, says it all. In the fourteenth century, in the Netherlands, a "modern or new devotion" arose as a lay movement of traditional monastic spirituality, challenging the dominant vision of religion. Certainly more late medieval (Catholic) than reformed (Protestant) in their ambiance and interests, the participants within this movement developed a way of devotion consonant with a vision of Christian perfection rooted in medieval monasticism, while providing an impetus for changes that would resonate strongly with the sensibilities of later Protestant reformers. Rather than rooting this movement too deeply in the medieval world or connecting it directly with the

Reformations that followed, however, this new spirituality stands on its own as a unique expression of Christian devotion.

On its most basic level, this movement reacted against the rigorous and academic intellectualism of so-called medieval scholasticism, on one hand, and the more radical spirituality of the Rhineland mystics, on the other. The great scholastics, or schoolmen, reveled in dialectics—the art of theological debate—and the pursuit of truth by means of philosophical argument about the deep questions of life. By contrast, in the school of theology associated particularly with Meister Eckhart (c. 1260–1329), perhaps the most famous of the Rhineland mystics, the soul proceeds by the negative way (via negativa) of imageless contemplation to union with God. Between these two extremes, the Modern Devotion charted a course along a "middle ground." The "new devout," as they were sometimes called, sought to establish a new devotion for the common person based on an interior transformation, reforming the soul and rejuvenating the spirit. The practical mystics of this new devotion viewed their movement as a return to a more ancient monastic tradition that combined a religion of the heart with acts of loving service to others in imitation of Jesus.

Brothers and Sisters of the Common Life

Most scholars attribute this new movement to Geert Groote (1340–1384), a Dutch canon lawyer who became an itinerant missionary and preacher. In consequence of a spiritual conversion in 1374 he gave his home to a group of women who styled themselves "Sisters of the Common Life." He became the director of the first houses of the "Brothers of the Common Life" in Deventer, gathering and training many disciples prior to his premature death to the plague in 1384. The spirituality of these groups of devout lay people was marked by their common life, voluntary association, sturdy doctrinal orthodoxy, and emphasis on humility and love in the pursuit of holiness.

Modeling their style of life after that of the earliest Christian communities depicted in the Acts of the Apostles, these "brothers and sisters" lived together and held all things in common. They subsisted by the work of their own hands and lived in simplicity. While they observed a basic rue of life, the devout refused to take lifelong vows. They advanced no peculiar doctrinal positions and required no confession of faith other than that of the universal church. They engaged in classic spiritual practices to cultivate virtue, giving particular attention to engagement with scripture in their common life, explication of the gospel among their neighbors (a practice described as "collation"), and mutual confession in the intimacy of small groups. Two years after Groote's death, a group of brothers organized a monastic community based on the Rule of Augustine—technically known as the Windesheim Congregation of Canons Regular—and devoted themselves to the principals of surrender to God, humility of spirit, manual labor, and virtuous living.

Thomas à Kempis
Born in the village of Kempen in the German Rhineland, Thomas à Kempis (c. 1380–1471)—also known as Thomas Hemerken—spent most of his life in the Netherlands promoting the spiritual vision of the Modern Devotion. At thirteen he left home to study at the Brothers of the Common Life school in Deventer, an institution established by Geert Groote's successor, Florent Radewijns. Thomas was so impressed with the authenticity of this community, and its faithful witness and commitment to spiritual ideals, that he immediately joined the "gathering," as it was called in Dutch. In 1399, he entered an Augustinian monastery three miles from Zwolle—a formal monastic community under the jurisdiction of the Brothers—where his elder brother, Jan, served as prior. He would spend the rest of his life at the Agnietenberg Priory (Mount St. Agnes), professing his vows in 1408, accepting ordination as a priest in 1413, and becoming sub-prior in 1425. In this capacity he served as the primary teacher of the novices and probably finalized his work on *The Imitation of Christ.*

The pattern of Thomas's life remained remarkably unchanged throughout the years. He devoted most of his time to meditation, reflection, prayer, reading, training the new brothers, and copying manuscripts.

It is said that he copied the entire Bible as many as four times. His brothers noted how he preferred the quiet of his own room, where he could pray, meditate, and study. It was in this quiet space that he produced a small corpus of writings. In addition to *The Imitation of Christ*, Thomas wrote several other devotional works, including biographies (particularly lives of the saints), sermons, letters, and hymns. A deep desire to live as Jesus's apprentice runs throughout all of his works. He died in relative obscurity at Agnietenberg on August 8, 1471, having done all in his power to pattern his own life after that of Jesus. While the earliest manuscripts of *The Imitation of Christ* are anonymous, most scholars today assign authorial credit to Thomas, although it is only proper to say that this is still disputed. Regardless, Thomas could hardly have imagined how influential this devotional work would prove to be over so many years.

The Form of *The Imitation of Christ*

The Imitation of Christ was probably written between 1420 and 1427. The book's emphasis on affective devotion—the religion of the heart, the need for Jesus's disciples to pattern their lives after the servant ministry of their Master, and the quest for holiness through purity of intention and humility shape the primary contours of this volume. Originally written for novices of the Modern Devotion, the book employs simple language to describe the spiritual journey into the heart of God through devotion to Jesus. Thomas conveys his practical advice as a spiritual guide by means of plain words for plain people, an aspect of *The Imitation of Christ* that has appealed to readers for centuries. The work is divided into four books, which reflect the primary tenets of Thomas's vision of the Christian life and the spirituality of the emerging new devotion.

Thomas emphasizes the practical aspects of Christian discipleship and structures *The Imitation of Christ* to give proper attention to a "lived or practiced faith." Book I, "The Life of the Soul," encourages the reader to develop a religion of the heart, primarily by renouncing all those things that separate the disciple from God. Book II, "The Interior Life," emphasizes

God's reign in the life of the believer and the necessity of uniting heart and mind to Jesus in order to grow in grace. Book III, "The Comfort of the Heart," grounds the Christian life in love and grace. Here, Thomas introduces a dialogical style that creates a more intimate and relational dynamic for the reader. Book IV, "The Sacrament of Holy Communion," continues this dialogue, bringing the believer's spiritual journey to its culmination in the intimacy of the sacred meal. Brief chapters comprise each of these books, focusing on particular themes relevant to living the Christ-like life day by day.

Some students of *The Imitation of Christ* discern the three movements of the so-called mystical way in the ordering of the first three Books of this classic spiritual guide. Book I, in other words, reflects the "purgative way." In this initial stage, the seeker is stripped from attachment to worldly things and attitudes in an effort to purify the soul and draw closer to God. Contemplation or knowledge of God characterizes the second movement, the "illuminative way." This stage takes the proficient—the one who has detached from common barriers to God—into a more transcendent awareness of the reality and love of Jesus. The final stage of spiritual growth in the cultivation of holiness, the "unitive way," leads the soul closer and closer to God's self until the heart of the believer fully rests in the love and reign of God. This lifelong pilgrimage culminates in the image of the heavenly banquet, the feast anticipated in every celebration of Eucharist. The progress of the soul through these various movements entails unfolding, discovering, and reclaiming the image of Jesus. Thomas emphasizes the practical aspects of this process.

The Spirituality of *The Imitation of Christ*

The Imitation of Christ reflects the most characteristic features of the spirituality of the Modern Devotion out of which this great work emerged. It focuses on the person of Jesus, the centrality of scripture, the importance of the heart, and the pursuit of holiness.

Living in Jesus. Thomas orients his spirituality around the person and work of Jesus. Like St. Paul, he conceives authentic Christian life as participation in Jesus. In Thomas's medieval context, the image of the cross dominated the world. God unites faithful Christians with Jesus in his sacrificial death in order to unite them with Jesus in a resurrection like his. Thomas advocates cruciform lives that await God's glory.

Engaging Scripture. Thomas understands his faith through the lens of the Bible. There are over seven hundred references to scripture in the original Latin edition of *The Imitation of Christ.* It is not too much to say that Thomas was a man of one book. He made the Bible his constant companion; *The Imitation of Christ,* on one level, is nothing other than a commentary on the Word of God. He advocates a biblical spirituality.

Forming the Heart. Thomas elevates an affective spirituality. He sees the heart as the spiritual center of the human being. He is careful, however, to avoid the cultivation of a heart turned in on itself; authentic Christians reach out to others with compassion and mercy. God shapes Christ-like dispositions in the heart of those who seek to love God and neighbor. Thomas advocates heart religion.

Pursuing Holiness. Thomas emphasizes holiness as the goal of the Christian journey. While forgiveness provides the foundation for human well-being and reconciliation with God, the authentic Christian pursues perfection in love, or holiness of heart and life. Those who are holy reflect the character of Jesus in their actual lives, giving evidence of their faith through active love. Thomas advocates a spirituality of holiness.

This spirituality also emphasizes practices that shape dispositions. Among these practices, of course, imitation stands out as the most critical. Imitation implies much more than simply mimicking Jesus; it means having his mind and spirit. Thomas devotes an entire Book to another practice in which all the other practices converge—Eucharist. The act of sharing in the sacred meal provides the paradigm and the means to experience abundant life. Likewise, *The Imitation of Christ* revolves around two dispositions that, for Thomas, define the journey into Christ-likeness and the ultimate meaning of life found in communion with God—humility and purity.

Two Formative Practices

One primary question dominates *The Imitation of Christ*: How does the authentic Christian follow Jesus? Thomas concludes that one can only answer this question in light of the practices that constitute the life of a faithful disciple. In a contemporary reflection on the meaning of practices, contemporary theologian Dr. Craig Dykstra offers this important insight that resonates well with Thomas's vision:

> Christian practices are not activities we do to make something spiritual happen in our lives. Nor are they duties we undertake to be obedient to God. Rather, they are patterns of communal action that create openings in our lives where the grace, mercy, and presence of God may be made known to us. They are places where the power of God is experienced. In the end, these are not ultimately our practices but forms of participation in the practice of God.[1]

The title of Thomas's classic devotional treatise identifies the primary practice of the Christian from his point of view—imitation of Christ.

Imitation

What did Thomas actually mean by the imitation of Christ? No doubt he had been greatly influenced by a more literal understanding of this concept as it had been developed earlier in the medieval period. Bernard of Clairvaux (1090–1153), the great Cistercian preacher of the twelfth century, for example, developed the practice of devotion to the "sacred humanity" of Jesus. This involved the point-by-point meditation on consecutive scenes from the life of Jesus. A century later, Francis of Assisi (c. 1181–1226) devoted himself to a literal, contemplative imitation of events in the life of Jesus. Both these great figures yearned for the human face and heart of God. The cross, in particular, and the five wounds of Jesus fascinated them both. In 1224, when Francis manifested the wounds of Jesus in his own body, many interpreted this as a sign of his full conformity to Jesus in a very literal sense. But all this raises the larger question of how we regard Jesus, in fact, as a model. Is a more literal mimicry of the historical Jesus what Thomas has in mind as he guides others in the imitation of Christ?

While it is important to be honest about the formative nature of this more literal tradition of imitation and this language of Christian devotion, the evidence concerning Thomas seems to point in a different and more nuanced direction. In 1 Corinthians 11:1, St. Paul admonishes his followers to "be imitators of me, as I am of Christ." To imitate Christ—to have the same mind in you that was in Christ (Philippians 2:5), to grow into the measure of the full stature of Jesus (Ephesians 4:13), to be a letter of Jesus written on the tablet of the human heart (2 Corinthians 3:3)—meant to become like Jesus in his obedience, humility, love, and service, qualities that were part and parcel of the portrait of Jesus in the Gospels. Many of the later Christian devotional writers preferred the Pauline language of "conformity to Christ" to the more literal "imitation of Christ." Despite the fact that Thomas seems to employ some of the imagery and language of the "literalists," he already seems to be moving in the direction of a much larger vision. These two views—the model to be outwardly imitated in a more literal sense and the inward patterning of a Christ-like character realized in heart and life—converge for Thomas in his vision of sacramental practice.

Eucharist

Every time the Christian community gathers around the Table of the Lord to celebrate the sacrament, it both imitates Jesus and seeks greater conformity to him. In a unique way, both elements of the Christian calling coalesce in this meal. Thomas devotes an entire Book to concerns related to the Sacrament, teaching his readers about the depth of its significance and its formative effect on the lives of believers. It is interesting that he continues the dialogical style introduced in Book III—a conversation, if you will, between Jesus and the disciple—in order to expound the spiritual meaning of this intimate event. He covers a wide range of topics, including a proper reverence of and preparation for the meal; the Sacrament as a memorial of Jesus's death and a sign and means of grace; the Table of Blessing as a place of divine–human encounter rooted in God's goodness, grace, and love. He advocates frequent celebration of this meal, something he considers to be absolutely essential to the Christian walk, a place above all others where the soul is united to and dwells in communion with God through Jesus.

While Thomas does not dwell on the more detailed elements of eucharistic practice, several aspects of the meal are noteworthy in terms of the formative effect of their imitation. In the context of the Upper Room Passover Meal, Jesus requested that his disciples repeat these actions in remembrance of him. This so-called *anamnesis*—the Greek word for remembrance—means to remember something in such a way that it becomes real in the present moment. The imitated actions of Jesus at the table bring him to life anew, as it were, in the hearts and minds of the faithful. Moreover, the actions of the Eucharist—taking, blessing, breaking, and giving—form the followers of Jesus in ways that lead to their greater conformity to his image. At each celebration of Holy Communion, the community of faith is taken, blessed, broken, and given—like Jesus—for the life of the world. In all these ways, the practice of Eucharist shapes those who seek to imitate Christ.

Two Essential Dispositions

Practices form dispositions. Thomas rediscovered the cultivation of virtue in his own day, and the concept of dispositions permeates *The Imitation of Christ*. All of us have certain predispositions, aspects of our personality or products of our nurture that predispose us to feel, think, or act in particular ways. For example, a child raised in a racist environment might practice discrimination on the basis of race as an adult. It is possible, however, to learn new ways of feeling, thinking, and acting, to shape certain dispositions in our hearts through intentional practice. St. Paul described these virtues as fruits of the Spirit: "love, joy, peace, patience, kindness, generosity, faithfulness, gentleness, and self-control" (Galatians 5:22–23a). In medieval theology, four cardinal virtues (temperance, fortitude or courage, prudence, and justice) and three higher theological virtues (faith, hope, and love) constituted the seven great virtues attested to in scripture and other traditions of morality. In *The Imitation of Christ*, though, Thomas emphasized two dispositions, in particular, both of which he viewed as essential to the formation of Christian character—humility and purity.

Humility

The disposition or virtue of humility is profoundly relational. Humility is defined primarily in terms of one's relationship with God and others. The humble acknowledge that everything they are and have comes from God. All abilities and accomplishments, to say nothing of life itself, God offers freely as gifts. Humility is grounded in our acknowledgment that we are totally dependent on God. Thomas enunciates this central theme throughout *The Imitation of Christ*. In dialogue with Jesus, the disciple confesses, "I am your lowest servant—so impotent and contemptible. You know, O Lord, that I am nothing, have nothing, and can do nothing. You alone are good, just, and holy. You can do all things" (III.3). True self-understanding—another primary and related theme—is the key, therefore, to the cultivation of a humble spirit. At the very outset of this devotional guide for the Christian walk, Thomas links this central point to a biblical admonition: "True self-knowledge is the highest and most profitable discovery in life. Do not think of yourself, therefore, more highly than you ought and always think well and highly of others" (I.2).

Given this paramount concern, Thomas shows great disdain for anything that engenders pride because this disposition, the opposite of humility, is the root of all sin. He demonstrates his conviction repeatedly that pride creates an insurmountable barrier between ourselves and God, a chasm that only God can bridge. Since the sin of pride turns us away from our greatest good, we often need to be shocked out of our complacency and false sense of self-importance. Pride "defaces your soul," claims Thomas. "The humble enjoy continuous peace, but envy, anger, and malice fester in the hearts of the proud" (I.6). This disease must be rooted out at all costs for it is the nemesis of the child of God. "Always be prepared to battle your pride," Thomas observes, "for it stands to your left and your right as a perennial enemy that never rests" (II.9). According to Thomas, however, no force in the universe is stronger than an intimate relationship with the God of love that forms a spirit of humility in the believer.

Purity

In the Sermon on the Mount, Jesus proclaimed: "Blessed are the pure in heart, for they shall see God" (Matthew 5:8). Thomas identifies purity as another disposition of critical importance in the soul's progress to God. He speaks most frequently in *The Imitation of Christ* of "purity of intention," a concept that relates most directly to the heart. The earliest Christians understood that, if those things that God commands are only done outwardly, and not inwardly—in the heart—such actions remain far removed from God's intentions. On the other hand, if the intention is pure, despite a less than perfect implementation, the disciple comes close to God. In his description of the pilgrim journey into the heart of God's love, Bernard of Clairvaux gave eloquent expression to this understanding of the purified heart: "O pure and sacred love! O sweet and pleasant affection! O pure and sinless intention of the will, all the more sinless and pure since it frees us from the taint of selfish vanity, all the more sweet and pleasant, for all that is found in it is divine."[2] Purity of intention implies a will attuned to God's own will and holiness. It consists of seeking the true end of our human existence, seeking to find and to fulfill God's will in everything, having God first and foremost in our thoughts, feelings, and actions.

When Thomas describes simplicity and purity as the two wings that enable the soul to soar (II.4), he directs the reader's attention to the heights of holiness achieved by those whose hearts and wills are firmly fixed on God. In the ancient Collect for Purity in the liturgy of the Church of England's *Book of Common Prayer*, the faithful pray for God to cleanse the thoughts of their hearts in order to make it possible for them to perfectly love God and worthily magnify God's holy name. A couple centuries after the publication of *The Imitation of Christ*, the reformed drafters of the Westminster Shorter Catechism (1647) described the glorification and enjoyment of God as the fundamental purposes of humanity. Purity of intention enables the child of God to love and glorify God to the fullest measure. Those who have purity of heart are free and filled with joy, as Thomas exclaims:

> If you intend and seek nothing but the will of God and the good of your neighbor, you will be truly free.... When you are good and pure, you see and understand all things from the right perspective. The condition of your inner self determines how you judge everything around you. If there is any joy in this world, surely the pure in heart possess it.
>
> (II.4)

This spirituality has shaped the lives of many Christians over the past six centuries. Soon after his religious conversion, Ignatius of Loyola (1491–1556), founder of the Society of Jesus (Jesuits), devoted a year to the study of *The Imitation of Christ* in hopes of following in Jesus's footsteps more closely. It is probably during this period that he prepared his famous *Spiritual Exercises*, a manual of arms for those who sought to imitate Jesus. John Newton (1725–1807), author of the familiar hymn *Amazing Grace*, associated his conversion with *The Imitation of Christ* as well. A horrendous storm had overtaken his ship on the open seas while he was reading *The Imitation of Christ*. Struck by Thomas's emphasis on the fragile nature of life, Newton gave his life to the God of grace. Dietrich Bonhoeffer (1906–1945), a Lutheran pastor martyred as a consequence of his discipleship, had been reading *The Imitation of Christ* the night before the Nazis led him to his execution at the end of the Second World War. Dag Hammarskjöld (1905–1961), secretary general of the United Nations, left his copy of the book with a friend as he embarked or a plane that would later crash in the dark of night. His oath of office was tucked in its pages with an affirmation of the duty to serve others. Ironically, Thomas Merton (1915–1968), one of the spiritual giants of the twentieth century, began reading *The Imitation of Christ* at the suggestion of a Hindu monk. He later noted its impact on his life. Like so many others, Pope John Paul I (1912–1978) had been reading this devotional classic in the Vatican at the time of his death.

John Wesley's Translation

John Wesley (1703–1791), founder of the Methodist movement, attests to the important role *The Imitation of Christ* played in his own spiritual pilgrimage. In the famous journal account of his evangelical conversion on May 24, 1738, he reflected on the formative influences of his earlier life that led up to this critical event. In 1725, the year of his ordination as a deacon in the Church of England, he started reading *The Imitation of Christ* and "began to see that true religion was seated in the heart, and that God's law extended to all our thoughts, as well as words and actions." In a similar reflective moment, in his *Plain Account of Christian Perfection* (1766) Wesley quotes Thomas directly. He recalls his discovery that "'simplicity of intention and purity of affection' are the 'wings of the soul' without which she can never ascend to the mount of God"[3] (Para. 3). It is most likely that he first read this work in the English translation by George Stanhope, retitled *The Christian's Pattern*, first published in 1698.[4]

Because Wesley was critical of some aspects of *The Imitation of Christ*, he decided to prepare his own translation in 1735. He used several Latin editions of the work and other English translations, revised his own work extensively, and produced what he considered to be a more literal but up-to-date version of the text. After the birth of the Methodist movement in 1738–39, he produced an abridgement of the work that he recommended to his followers for the enhancement of their devotional life. In 1741, he published a more fully revised *Extract of The Christian's Pattern*, reduced to two-thirds of its original length and produced in a less expensive form. He carried this volume with him wherever he traveled as a close companion to his Bible. This present edition of *The Imitation of Christ* is based on Wesley's translation of the extracted work.

Wesley abridged the original work markedly (a comparison of the original work, Wesley's abridged edition, and this present volume can be found at the end of the book, p. 179), omitting 22 of the original 114 chapters and revising the remaining material with an eye for greater concision and less redundancy. Some of Wesley's deletions reflect theological differences or aspects of Christian tradition foreign to his own practice or not germane to his own time. He deletes full chapters, for example, on "God's Grace Is Not Given to the Earthly Minded" (III.53), "Monastic Life" (I.17), and "Acquiring Patience in the Fight Against Concupiscence" (III.12) for these kinds of reasons. Other chapters, like "Contempt for All Earthly Honor" (III.41) and "Temporal Sufferings Should Be Borne Patiently" (III.18), simply reiterate themes fully examined, in his view, elsewhere in the work.

Since this present edition is based on Wesley's translation, all his omissions are followed, including his abbreviations of the chapters. Occasionally, he forms single chapters of his own by combining material from two revised chapters of the original work, as is the case with regard to I.12/I.13, I.18/19, I. 21/22, and II.7/8. In only one case does Wesley split the material of an original chapter into two separate segments (IV.13). Despite a fairly heavy editorial hand, he retains all the chapters in Book II and omits only three chapters each from Books I and IV. He deletes three times the amount of material from the lengthy Book III as from the other three Books combined. Since this volume is meant to be an introduction to *The Imitation of Christ*, an even larger number of chapters have been omitted (43), primarily from Book III as well, reducing the original work still further. Enumeration of chapters in this volume follows Wesley's style, with a Roman numeral indicating the Book and an Arabic numeral indicating the chapter. In the citations above, this style of citation refers to the original text, whereas all subsequent references follow Wesley's scheme.

Editorial work of this nature entails an extremely subjective process. I have made an attempt, however, to retain the central emphases of *The Imitation of Christ*, identifying some of the great gems of Thomas's spiritual teaching. Further, I have "modernized" the language of Wesley's extract in order to make this material more accessible to contemporary readers. Whenever I have introduced changes to the text, I have tried diligently to retain the meaning and emphasis of Wesley's extract. An example drawn from Book I, chapter 5 on "Scripture," comparing Wesley's extract and my own modernization, illustrates the direction I have taken with regard to the text.

> Truth, not eloquence, is to be sought for in Holy Scripture. All Scripture is to be read by the same spirit wherewith it was written. We ought to read plain and devout books as willingly as high and profound ones. Let not the authority of the writer, whether he be of great or small learning, but the love of pure truth, draw thee to read. Search not who spake this, but mark what was spoken.
>
> (I.5 WESLEY TRANSLATION)

> Seek the truth rather than the beauty of the Holy Scriptures. Attempt to read Scripture in the same spirit in which it was written (Romans 15:4). Immerse yourself in practical, devotional literature with as much eagerness as you embrace lofty and academic works. Let the

love of simple truth, rather than the reputation or the authority of the author, motivate your reading (1 Corinthians 2:4). Do not pay as much attention to who wrote the book as you do to what the author actually has to say.

(I.5 MODERNIZATION)

This comparison demonstrates a number of important principles that guided the modernization of the text. I have frequently changed passive expressions to active voice in order to create a greater sense of movement in the narrative. Similarly, I have often defaulted to a "second person" mode instead of "third person." An excerpt from Book I, chapter 3 illustrates this approach. Wesley's original reads: "He is truly great, that is great in love.... He is truly wise, that accounteth all earthly things as dung, that he may win Christ. And he is truly learned that doth the will of God, and forsaketh his own will." The modernized text admonishes: "You are truly great if you love greatly.... You are truly wise if you regard all earthly things as rubbish, in order that you may gain Christ. You are truly learned if you do the will of God and forsake your own foolish ways." My hope is that this direct address engages the reader more fully.

I am strongly committed to the use of inclusive language in all my writing and teaching. Wherever I noted possible changes for the purpose of greater inclusivity that were not destructive, in my judgment, to the flow of the text, I have made them. I have removed linguistic archaisms such as "wherewith," "thee," and "spake," as illustrated in this particular instance. Whenever I have been able to identify a clear biblical allusion or a direct quotation, I have employed the New Revised Standard Version translation, unless otherwise noted. On a number of occasions I have taken greater license with the original text in an effort to bring greater clarity to the original meaning. In the instance of comparison just offered, the modernization is slightly longer than the original; in other contexts, the opposite is the case. My hope is that contemporary readers will find this new version of The Imitation of Christ both relevant and applicable to their spiritual journey today.

Instructions to the Reader

John Wesley provides some helpful guidelines to the reader—his translation, actually, of a preface to a Latin edition of the work, was published in Cologne in 1682. These prefatory comments to the volume have stood the test of time. Follow his suggestions as you engage this book and apply the insights of *The Imitation of Christ* to your life.

It is impossible for readers to comprehend this devotional work fully unless they read it in such a manner as it deserves. Instead of heaping up commendations of it—which those who have read it do not want, and those who have not will not believe—I have formulated a few plain directions on how to read this, or indeed any other religious book.

Assign a particular time every day to read and ponder this book. If you miss the devotional time you have set apart for any reason, simply avail yourself of the next possible opportunity for it. When large portions of each day are so willingly given to other activities, is it too much to devote some little time daily for the improvement of your immortal soul?

Prepare yourself for reading by purity of intention, whereby you simply aim at your soul's benefit. In a short prayer, ask for God's grace to enlighten your understanding and to prepare your heart for receiving what you read. Pray that you may both know what God requires of you, and seriously resolve to translate God's will into action once you know it.

Do not read in a cursory or hasty way, but leisurely, seriously, and attentively. Permit yourself proper intervals and pauses to allow time for spiritual wisdom to sink in deeply. Stop frequently to journal about what you have read, and consider how to put it into practice. Moreover, let your reading be continued and regular, not rambling and haphazard. You will not be able to digest this material easily if you taste many dishes without fixing upon or being satisfied with any. It will serve you well, however, if you read over and over those passages that touch you most deeply and more closely affect your own practice or inclinations. Ponder those passages and inwardly digest them.

Foster an attitude or spirit that is consistent with what you read, otherwise it will prove empty and unprofitable. It will only enlighten your understanding without influencing your will or inflaming your affections. Therefore, intersperse pious aspirations to God and petitions for grace here and there. Also, collect particularly meaningful sayings or memorable pieces of advice; treasure them up in your memory to ponder in your heart. You can later draw these forth as arrows from a quiver against temptations and against this or that vice to which you are more particularly susceptible. They can also function as incitements to humility, patience, the love of God, or any other virtue.

Conclude every time of devotional reading with a short prayer to God. Ask God to preserve and nurture the good seed sown in your heart, that it may bring forth its fruit in due season. Do not think that this will take up too much of your time; no time could ever be put to better use.

BOOK I
The Life of the Soul

[1] Thomas à Kempis opens *The Imitation of Christ* with a direct quote from John's Gospel. He sets out a stark contrast here at the very beginning between darkness and light, a favorite theme in the Gospel as well. God is light, grace, and love. We see these amazing qualities in Jesus, are drawn to his light, and seek to reflect the light of God's love as the source of all life.

[2] We usually think of imitation in the sense of observing and replicating the behavior of some other person. Certainly, Thomas has this in mind as he enunciates the central theme of this devotional work. On its most basic level, imitation of Christ means to live a Christ-like life. But this means much more than simply mimicking Jesus. To use the image of St. Paul, it means "having the mind of Christ" (Philippians 2:5)—cultivating a spirit like that of Jesus. Thomas emphasizes actions, but he also draws our attention to an attitude or attribute that is well worth emulation—humility. Action that is Christ-like flows out of a spirit like that of Jesus.

[3] Thomas offers another set of contrasting images. In the same way that light stands over against darkness, the heart and the head also represent something of a tension in our spiritual quest. Thomas doesn't so much disparage the use of our minds as he guards against the dangerous elevation of the human intellect over all things. After all, the seed of pride—the antithesis of humility—is sewn first in the mind. Each of Thomas's terse statements provides a poignant illustration of an intellectual hubris that drives us from God. He advocates a heart religion that turns us away from the vanities of this world, from preoccupation with self and human achievement, and instead orients all life around the love and service of God and others. The Christian lives *in* but not *of* the world.

CHAPTER 1

☐ The Imitation of Christ

"Whoever follows me will never walk in darkness but will have the light of life" (John 8:12).[1] These are the words of Christ by which he advises you to imitate his life and his ways if you want to be truly enlightened and delivered from all blindness of heart. Therefore, let your chief endeavor be to reflect on the life of Jesus Christ.[2]

What good does it do to be able to discuss the mysteries of the Trinity if, lacking in humility, you displease God? Truly, education alone does not make people holy and just; but a virtuous life makes them dear to God. Is it not better for you to feel contrition than to know how to define the term? What would it profit you if you knew the whole Bible by heart and the sayings of all the philosophers, but you never experienced the grace and love of God (1 Corinthians 13:2)? Vanity of vanities! All is vanity (Ecclesiastes 1:2). Loving and serving God is more important than anything else.[3]

1 Thomas provides variations on the central theme of St. Paul's text from 1 Corinthians: "Knowledge puffs up, but love builds up." A huge chasm stretches between the two statements "I know about God" and "I know God." According to Thomas, an intimate relationship with the God of love that forms humility in the believer characterizes authentic Christian existence. Love, not knowledge, is the ultimate goal; Thomas points consistently to the self-giving love of Jesus.

2 Thomas explores the virtue, or disposition, of humility and connects it closely with wisdom. While many believe that knowledge leads to wisdom, life demonstrates clearly that those who know a lot sometimes do not use their knowledge in wise ways. How we use the knowledge we possess is more important than the knowledge itself. Wisdom and humility do not simply happen; rather, we must cultivate these dispositions, and *The Imitation of Christ* helps the disciple learn how to do this.

3 Many attribute the famous ancient Greek aphorism, "Know thyself," to the philosopher Socrates (c. 469–399 BCE). In Plato's *Dialogues*, the character of Socrates uses this maxim to motivate the reader to greater self-understanding in at least six of the conversations. The admonition to know oneself not only implies the need for deep introspection but also identifies one's proper place in relation to God—a posture of humility—as the key to all life. Thomas will return to the theme of self-knowledge repeatedly.

CHAPTER 2

☐ Humility

Do not focus all your energies simply on knowing things, for this quest can easily distract and deceive you. Intellectuals like to appear learned and to be called wise (1 Corinthians 8:1). But there are many aspects of knowledge that do nothing to promote your spiritual life. Those who focus all their attention on matters that have nothing to do with the welfare of the soul lack wisdom. Many desires leave the soul unsatisfied, but anyone with a pure conscience can face God with confidence.[1]

The more you know and the better you understand, the more acutely you will be judged, unless your life is all the more holy. Therefore, do not take pride in your learning and skill; rather, let the knowledge that God has given to you fill you with awe. If you think you know a lot, acknowledge that there are many more things about which you know nothing. Do not let your knowledge turn you into an arrogant person; rather, admit your own ignorance. Those who aspire to be wise seek to nurture a spirit of humility in their lives.[2]

True self-knowledge is the highest and most profitable discovery in life.[3] Do not think of yourself, therefore, more highly than you ought and always think well and highly of others (Romans 12:3).

1 Thomas believes that we apprehend the truth directly. Truth, in other words, authenticates itself; it does not need to be proven. He roots this concept in his understanding of a personal God who is Truth. We apprehend this Truth in the person of Jesus. God teaches us the truth through a relationship with the One who is the Truth.

2 Truth leads to peace, both with oneself and with others.

3 Thomas moves seamlessly from his discourse into prayer. Like the famous *Confessions* of the founding father of Latin Christianity and bishop of Hippo, St. Augustine (354–430), *The Imitation of Christ* is also essentially an act of prayer.

4 Thomas establishes one of his most famous principles: We are our own worst enemies. This need to get over ourselves, to acknowledge the barriers we construct for ourselves, and to break out of vicious cycles of self-destructive behavior, dominates the spiritual journey.

5 What a poignant and memorable portrait of the Christian life and its goals: We are truly great, wise, and learned if we love greatly, seek after Christ in all things, and do God's will.

CHAPTER 3

☐ Truth

Happy is the one to whom truth comes, not in elusive signs and words, but by an immediate communication of itself (Psalm 94:12).[1] Your own opinions and sense of things will often deceive you; little can be discerned through them.

All things come from the one Word and they reflect their Creator. This same One speaks directly to you. You cannot understand or judge correctly without God. If you embrace the source of all truth—if you trace all things back to Truth and see all things in it—then your heart will be undisturbed and you will be at peace with God.[2] O God, O eternal Truth, make me one with you in everlasting love. I am weary of reading and hearing; in you I find all that I desire. Let all creatures be silent before you. Speak to me, I pray.[3]

A pure, simple, and steadfast spirit is not fragmented, even when employed in many activities, because it does everything to the glory of God and seeks nothing for itself. Your most difficult battle in life is your effort to overcome yourself.[4] This ought to be your primary business—to conquer self and to advance in holiness daily.

You are truly great if you love greatly.... You are truly wise if you regard all earthly things as rubbish, in order that you may gain Christ (Philippians 3:8). You are truly learned if you do the will of God and forsake your own foolish ways.[5]

✚ The Wisdom Literature of the Hebrew Bible (the books of Job, Proverbs, Ecclesiastes, Psalms, and Song of Solomon) shaped Thomas in profound ways. Many of the scriptural allusions in *The Imitation of Christ* are drawn from these works. Thomas's own writing often has the feel of this genre of the ancient Near East. *The Imitation of Christ* is filled with pithy, direct advice, seeking to teach about God and virtue. As in this chapter, these statements often come across as "do's and don'ts," but Thomas's primary intention is to elevate proven practices that shape godly dispositions in life.

1 Prudence is one of the four so-called cardinal virtues. The term "cardinal" comes from the Latin word for hinge, implying that these virtues (also including justice, temperance, and courage) are the hinges of, or pivotal to, a moral life. Thomas Aquinas (1225–1274), the greatest theologian of the medieval church, provided the normative exposition of these virtues, as well as the theological virtues of faith, hope, and love, to form the seven virtues of medieval Christianity. Prudence is the ability to govern oneself by good sense.

2 Note the multiple references to wisdom and the string of allusions to the book of Proverbs. Thomas inextricably links wisdom, prudence, and humility.

3 The spirituality of Thomas is teleological; that is, it is oriented to a particular goal. He admonishes his readers to engage in practices that cultivate virtue because a virtuous life leads to happiness. John Wesley later developed this theme in a vision of the Christian life in which holiness meant happiness.

CHAPTER 4

☐ Prudence[1]

Do not give in to every impulse, but take time to carefully ponder these things according to the will of God.... If you want to be wise and perfect, do not give credence easily to everything you hear from others, because you know how frail your brothers and sisters in the human family can be (Genesis 8:21).

Do not be rash and cling to your own opinions, therefore, as if they were incontestable facts. If you desire wisdom, do not believe everything you hear and do not gossip each new piece of information to others without due consideration (Proverbs 17:9). Consult with wise and conscientious friends and seek to be instructed by those you hold in high esteem, rather than following your own inclinations (Proverbs 12:15). Practicing the good life cultivates godly wisdom (Proverbs 15:33) and provides experience in a wide range of affairs (Ecclesiastes 1:16).[2] Humility and submission to the things of God produce peace and contentment in the soul.[3]

✝ Immersion in scripture is a foundational means of grace. God's Word informs, forms, and transforms all who engage it with sincerity and serious expectation. It should be no surprise that a discussion of scripture appears so early in this devotional classic. The Christian practice of *lectio divina* (sacred reading), involving four distinct movements of reading, meditation, prayer, and contemplation, seeks to enhance the formative nature of Bible reading.

1 God speaks. Most of us, perhaps, do not think a lot about how God speaks, but Thomas wants to make sure we don't miss this significant aspect of God's way. God speaks all creation into being. The writer of John's Gospel describes Jesus as the Word. It is quite amazing, actually, to contemplate how God accommodates speech so that all can hear and understand. We often say that something really "speaks to me." Thomas's point is that God yearns to connect with us through words; God meets us in a myriad of ways through the Word.

2 Thomas's advice concerning how to read scripture is clear and simple: approach the Word with humility, seeking self-transformation—not just information.

CHAPTER 5

☐ Scripture

Seek the truth rather than the beauty of the Holy Scriptures. Attempt to read Scripture in the same spirit in which it was written (Romans 15:4). Immerse yourself in practical, devotional literature with as much eagerness as you embrace lofty and academic works. Let the love of simple truth, rather than the reputation or the authority of the author, motivate your reading (1 Corinthians 2:4). Do not pay as much attention to who wrote the book as you do to what the author actually has to say.

Every person's life comes to an end, but "all wisdom is from the Lord, and with God it remains forever" (Ecclesiasticus 1:1). God speaks to us in all kinds of ways, without discriminating against any.[1]

If you desire to profit from your study of the Word, read humbly, simply, and faithfully, and do not seek a reputation for being learned. Give willing and attentive consideration to the reflections of the saints in these matters; do not dismiss the perspective of the elders, for they had good reason to speak as they did.[2]

1 Spiritual maturity comes only to those who put their whole trust in God. Thomas suffers under no delusion that this is an easy, one-time accomplishment. In fact, a steady, intentional journey is the path enabling you to entrust your whole heart, mind, and soul to God. But the central question of life is this: To what or to whom do you entrust your life? To yourself, and you alone? Thomas insists that only those who, by God's grace, repeatedly entrust their days to God will find true happiness and peace to be their reliable pattern.

2 What damage does pride do to us? Given the fact that God has created us to live in relationships of love with all others, the most dangerous aspect of pride has to do with the way it disrupts our relationships. Essentially, pride makes genuine love impossible, and nothing could be more detrimental to the soul, walling us off from God's presence in others.

3 Thomas uses the metaphor of "disease" to discuss the pathology of pride. Pride only produces envy, anger, and malice—character traits that fester and poison the whole person—but humility leads to peace—putting one, in contrast, at "ease" in life. The answer to human pride may not be repressing it as much as entrusting it to God, with honesty and authenticity, accepting God's merciful forgiveness and moving forward with a new spirit.

CHAPTER 6

☐ Vanity and Pride

Only the foolish put their trust in people (Jeremiah 17:5). Do not be ashamed to serve others for the love of Jesus Christ or to be held in low esteem by those in this world. Guard yourself against a spirit of self-sufficiency; rather, trust and hope in God (Psalm 31:1). Do what lies in your power and God will assist your good intentions. Do not trust in your own knowledge or skill or that of other people (Jeremiah 9:23). Put your whole trust in the God who "opposes the proud, but gives grace to the humble" (James 4:6).[1]

Do not think yourself better than others or God might view you worse than them all. Do not take pride in your good deeds (Job 9:20), for the judgment of God concerning them is far different from the judgment of your peers. If there is any good at all in you, believe that there is much more in others. Whereas it does no harm to you if you esteem yourself less than others, it defaces your soul when you think that you are better than everyone else.[2] The humble enjoy continuous peace, but envy, anger, and malice fester in the hearts of the proud.[3]

1 Comparing ourselves to others and attempting to control them are the twin barriers to peace in life. The former alienates us from ourselves and the latter alienates us from others. Thomas advises that we steer clear of both.

2 In his time, Thomas was concerned about people who lived superficial lives. In our own time, it is so easy for us to get caught up in trifles and miss the most important realities of life. Suffering and pain often trigger concern about the deeper meaning of life. Sometimes these experiences exert a more powerful force than an act of will.

3 There are many English proverbial sayings similar to this. We think, for example, of the phrase attributed frequently to the famous football coach Knute Rockne (1888–1931): "When the going gets tough, the tough get going." But the play on words can mean the opposite: "When things get difficult, those who rely on their own strength quickly abandon the situation." Thomas wants to guard against this by encouraging us to seek the higher way. Animated by the same concern, Oswald Chambers (1874–1917), the noted Scottish minister and teacher, produced his classic devotional guide, *My Utmost for His Highest*.

4 God's grace and strength—not our own—are the keys to spiritual growth and victory.

CHAPTER 7

☐ Peace

How can you find peace in your own life if you immerse yourself in all those aspects of other people's lives that have nothing to do with you? How can you find peace for yourself if you are constantly meddling in the affairs of others and fail to examine your own heart regularly? "Blessed are the pure in heart, for they will see God" (Matthew 5:8) and enjoy much peace.[1]

It is so easy to become preoccupied with personal whims and passions and to get caught up in things that do not last. If you are not equally passionate about growing in grace and love day by day, you will always remain cold and indifferent to those things that are most important in life.[2]

If you focus your attention on God rather than yourself—and seek the highest good rather than the easiest path—then godly things will excite you more and more. Otherwise, whenever you encounter difficulties, you will simply seek escape through worldly pleasures.[3]

Life is sometimes like a battle. It requires great courage and endurance. So ask God to assist you and help will surely come. The One who has given you the opportunity to fight the good fight will provide all you need to obtain victory in the end. But do not entrust your growth in holiness to outward practices or you will quickly burn out trying to do it all on your own.[4]

1 Thomas examines one of the most unfortunate aspects of human brokenness. We are easily pulled in directions that lead us astray. Instead of following God's way, we choose paths that take us away from God and our true selves. Temptation is inescapable—but it can also draw us closer to God.

2 It is not always easy to know why we do the things we do. Our tendency to succumb to temptation has deep roots in our inner selves. We don't like to face this inner darkness, but it is the only way to spiritual health and true peace. Long before twelve-step programs of restoration, Thomas realized that people must admit they cannot control their compulsions, recognize that a higher power can give them strength, and examine the roots of their brokenness with the help of others. As St. Paul confessed: "I do not understand my own actions. For I do not do what I want, but I do the very thing I hate" (Romans 7:15).

3 Few people are able to experience trust in God if they do not have a vision of the goodness of God. Such a vision develops over time, especially for those who have not had the capacity to trust cultivation in their lives from an early age. We learn to trust others in life; our relationship with God is no different. Despite the fact that God is trustworthy in every way, many people find it hard to feel this or know it in the depths of their souls. Regardless, God's love remains steadfast and true.

CHAPTER 8

☐ Temptation

Temptation affords an opportunity for you to embrace total dependence on God. You will always be tempted in this world. According to Job, "Do not human beings have a hard service on earth ... ?" (7:1). Guard yourself, therefore, against temptation. Watch in prayer so that you will not be deceived.... No one is secure from temptation in this life.[1]

Only patience and humility, however, can conquer the power of temptation and evil in your life. You can avoid temptation and flee from it, but unless you deal effectively with the roots of temptation, your own efforts will profit very little. The temptations will simply return and make you feel worse than before. But if you wait patiently and rely upon God's help, you will be able to overcome them more easily. Do not beat yourself up at each failure or try to pull yourself up on the basis of your own strength when you fall. Put your confidence in God.[2]

All temptation begins with an irresolute mind and a lack of trust in God.[3] If you are careless and wavering, you will be tossed to and fro on the waves like a ship without a rudder. In the same way that fire tempers iron, triumph over temptation demonstrates your strength of character. Often you do not know what you are capable of unless you are tested.

(continued on page 19)

4   Understanding this simple process can be so helpful: thought, imagination, delight, consent. All people experience this subtle progression into sin in life. Given this perspective on how temptation works, it makes sense that "nipping the thought in the bud" is the best way to avoid falling into the trap.

5   Thomas provides no "one size fits all" remedy for temptation. He recognizes human diversity and he understands that each person must find his or her own antidote to this spiritual pathology. One thing remains clear: Everyone must deal with this issue, and entrusting one's life to God is the key to success. "Let go and let God," as it is often said.

6   As Thomas concludes his discussion of this serious matter, he sounds a note of hope. Despite the failures, cycles, entanglements, and complexities related to our bad decisions in life, God remains faithful to us, and there is a special place in God's heart for those who remain humble through it all.

Be particularly careful at the beginning of temptation. Do not let the enemy enter the door of your heart.... Temptation works in this way: First, an unrighteous thought creeps into your mind. Next, your imagination takes hold of the idea. Then you begin to delight in the thought of the action. Finally, you consent.[4] Little by little the enemy secures entrance into your heart if you do not resist at the very beginning. Over time, the less you resist, the weaker you become, and the enemy gains strength in your heart. Some suffer the greatest temptation at the beginning of their journey, while others struggle at the very end. For still others, temptation seems to be their constant companion along the way.[5]

But in the midst of your struggles with temptation, never despair.[6] Pray to God all the more fervently. As St. Paul says: "No testing has overtaken you that is not common to everyone. God is faithful, and he will not let you be tested beyond your strength, but with the testing he will also provide the way out so that you may be able to endure it" (1 Corinthians 10:13). Humble yourself before God in every trial and temptation, for God will save and exalt the humble in spirit.

✣ Some critics of Thomas erroneously level the charge of "salvation by works" against him. On one hand, he grasps the Christian Scriptures' vision that followers of Jesus work out their own salvation with fear and trembling (Philippians 2:12), the source of this charge. We work out our salvation as we meet God in scripture, prayer, worship, and service. We actively fight sin, rather than sitting back passively to await some divine intervention. On the other hand, Thomas maintains that disciples of Jesus root their lives in him and not on their own efforts. He grasps the full statement of St. Paul to the fledgling community at Philippi: "Work out your own salvation; ... for it is God who is at work in you, enabling you both to will and to work for his good pleasure" (Philippians 2:12–13). So "works of charity" are the fruit of a life rooted in Jesus.

1 Perhaps this concept in *The Imitation of Christ* inspired one of the most famous ideas of the sainted founder of the Missionaries of Charity in Calcutta, Mother Teresa (1910–1997), that we can do no great things, only small things with great love. These opening sentences related to "loving action" merit prolonged meditation. If this sentiment shared by Teresa and Thomas is true, living out this basic principle will change your life.

2 Love is the antidote to envy and pride.

3 A note of pathos characterizes this ultimate appeal. Thomas longs for everyone to discover the transformative quality of God's love. Why? Because whenever we abide in this love and seek to reciprocate this love in all we do, as Charles Wesley sings, "the ray shall rise into a sun, the drop shall swell into a sea" (*Hymns on the Lord's Supper* [1745], Hymn 101, stanza 4).

CHAPTER 9

☐ Works of Charity

Outward works without love have little ultimate value (1 Corinthians 13:3). But whatever you do for love's sake—whether large or small— will bear great fruit. God values how much love you pour into each action, rather than how much you do. You do a lot whenever you love a lot.[1]

If true and perfect love motivates all that you do, then you will seek nothing for your own benefit (Philippians 2:21). The glory of God will be your whole delight. Loving persons envy no one because they are not seeking their own satisfaction. They do not take pride in the things they do, because they seek the righteousness of God in all things (Psalm 17:15).[2] They do not attribute goodness to any person, but refer it all to God, who is the source of every good and perfect gift (James 1:17). Those who are faithful ultimately abide in God's goodness and love. Oh, if you had but one spark of true love, you would certainly discern that all earthly things are full of vanity![3]

✞ Early English translations of Galatians 5:22, in which St. Paul enumerates the fruits of the Spirit, identify "long-suffering" as the fourth disposition of mature Christians. More recent translations render the same term "patience." Rather than being "quick tempered," the person who has the spirit of Jesus exhibits patience towards others. Through a series of rhetorical questions, Thomas provides multiple perspectives on the so-called Golden Rule: "Do to others as you would have them do to you" (Luke 6:31). He demonstrates that true religion and spiritual maturity are all about relationships. Loving relationships are built on patience and grace.

1 Everyone has faults, carries heavy burdens, and needs the strength and wisdom of others. Such a perspective leads to humility and a healthy sense of interdependence. No one can go it alone in the journey of life—we need one another and need to be honest about how much we depend on one another. Not only are those who imitate Jesus totally dependent on God, they are also dependent on others to help them grow toward the goal of love. As a member of the *devotio moderna*, Thomas learned that authentic Christianity necessarily entails community. As John Wesley would later maintain, there is no such thing as a solitary Christian.

CHAPTER 10

☐ Long-Suffering

Bear the defects and infirmities of others with patience because you may have many faults that others have to endure (1 Thessalonians 5:14). If you find it difficult to become the person you hope to be, is it right for you to bend other people to your own will? You want them to be perfect, but you cannot amend your own faults. You want them to be chastised severely, but you will not correct yourself.... Is it right for you to relate to others in a way that is different from the way you would have them relate to you?

God has created you in such a way that you learn important life lessons when you bear the burdens of others (Galatians 6:2). No one is faultless. No one is without burdens in life. No one is self-sufficient. None are wise enough for themselves.[1] Therefore, you ought to bear with others, comfort, help, instruct, and support others in the journey through life. The way in which you respond to the adversity of others demonstrates your own virtue. These moments in life reveal your true character.

✝ Saints are not necessarily extraordinary people; rather, they are ordinary people who do extraordinary things with God. They reflect the loving presence of God in their lives. They demonstrate their holiness with intentionality, choosing to love God and neighbor day-by-day. They exemplify what it means to imitate Christ, offering the best invitation into godliness—a life that shows it is possible to become like Jesus. Those with eyes to see will be inspired to enter the same good journey.

1 These are specific titles given to those within the communion of saints—those great people of faith who have died and now live with God. Apostles (from the Greek word meaning "a person who is sent out") carried the message of God's love out into the world. Martyrs (from the Greek word meaning "witness") sacrificed their lives for the faith. Confessors boldly declared their faith in the face of opposition and hardship. In the early church, virgins were women who were betrothed mystically to Christ and dedicated their lives exclusively to the service of the church. Today we might simply describe them as chaste single people, like nuns and monks living a consecrated life.

2 Thomas provides a stunning portrait of those honored for the way they imitated Christ. They immersed themselves in the means of grace through classical spiritual disciplines, particularly prayer and fasting. Through these exterior practices they cultivated the interior dispositions of perfect love, purity of intention, and unity with God—they were "participants of the divine nature" (2 Peter 1:4). Thomas tends to envisage "perfection" along these lines.

CHAPTER 11

☐ Holy Forebears

Consider the inspirational lives of the saints—in whom true perfection and religion shined brightly (Hebrews 11)—and you will see how far you are from the highest standards of holy living.... These pilgrims and friends of Jesus served the Lord in hunger and thirst, in cold and nakedness, in work and weariness, in vigils and fasting, in persecutions and affliction.

Apostles, martyrs, confessors, virgins,[1] and all those who sought to follow in the footsteps of Jesus committed themselves to life with God. Rather than seeking fame and fortune in this world, they sought "to store up ... treasures in heaven" (Matthew 6:20).... They offered their prayers frequently and fervently to God. They fasted rigorously. They pursued perfect love with great zeal and care. They waged war against spiritually debilitating sins. They cultivated purity of intention in their quest for unity with God. They devoted all their energy to the pursuit of spiritual perfection, endeavored to pray without ceasing, and filled their days with the contemplation of God.[2]

(continued on page 27)

3 Thomas employs a potent rhetorical device. Each statement contrasts a worldly appearance with a godly reality. The godly person is poor, but rich; destitute, but refreshed; a stranger, but a friend; and nothing, but precious. These affirmations demonstrate how the gospel turns the world upside down.

4 Thomas describes persons who seek to be like Jesus in a most succinct manner.

5 This prayer combines prayer and work, contemplation and action, the interior and the exterior life. It reflects a holistic vision of Christian discipleship, emphasizing the central metaphor of journey.

6 If you immerse yourself in works of piety (like prayer and Bible study) and works of mercy (like compassion and justice), undertaken in partnership with God, you will move closer to the goal of perfect love day-by-day. One's journey into God need not be a daily exercise in failure. Heart-change actually can happen.

They renounced all riches, dignities, honors, friends, and associates (Matthew 19:29). They had no interest in the things of this world. They lived as simply as they could. They were poor in earthly things, but rich in grace. They may have appeared destitute, but they were refreshed inwardly by constant communion with God. They were strangers to the world, but intimate with God. To themselves they seemed of little consequence, and were despised by the world, but God viewed them as precious children.[3] They lived in genuine humility, walked in love and patience, and progressed daily in their pilgrimage of faith.[4]

Every day you ought to pray, "Help me, O God, to be pure in my intention and active in your holy service. Grant me now, this very day, to begin perfectly, for I am only taking the first steps in my journey toward spiritual health."[5] "Gird up your loins" (Job 38:3) against the assaults of the devil, get your natural appetites under control, and you will more easily bridle all the temptations of the flesh. Above all things, avoid idleness; rather, read, write, pray, meditate, and work for the good of others.[6] "Blessed is that slave whom his master will find at work when he arrives. Truly I tell you, he will put that one in charge of all his possessions" (Luke 12:43–44).

☨ Jesus spent much time in solitude. It was necessary for him to retreat from the normal, sometimes chaotic, round of life to be alone with God. Through solitude he learned how to abide in God, and we would do well to imitate this practice. We live our lives sometimes at a frenetic pace. It is important to stop, ponder, rest, and listen, and to receive the restorative energy of silence. A cacophony of sound impinges on us every day, bombarding us with demands, claims, and false promises. Silence stills the soul and makes it possible to hear the "still, small voice of God" more clearly.

1 Thomas offers sound advice to those who wish to practice a spiritual discipline such as solitude. Such a discipline presents challenges at first. But once the rhythm is established, it liberates us from the silly pattern of insisting on our own way and brings great joy.

2 Those things that are most meaningful to us in life are often charged emotionally. Thomas appears to be unafraid of emotion; he embraces the emotive qualities of a life lived in intimacy with God.

CHAPTER 12

☐ Solitude and Silence

Seek suitable times (Ecclesiastes 3:1) to retreat into solitude and contemplate God.... The Psalmist admonishes: "When you are disturbed, do not sin; ponder it on your beds, and be silent" (4:4). You will find those things in solitude that the world steals from you. The more time you spend in quiet prayer, the more you will benefit from it; the less time you devote to solitude, the more it will feel like a burden. If you embrace a pattern of prayer that includes solitude and silence early in your spiritual journey, by the end of your life it will be a dear friend and pleasant comfort.[1]

Your soul learns and profits from the hidden truths of Scripture through silent reflection and quiet meditation. The flood of tears that such practice elicits bathes and cleanses the soul. It draws the soul into an intimate relationship with the Creator.[2]

"I lift up my eyes to the hills—from where will my help come?" (Psalm 121:1). Your help comes from the Lord your God. Pray to God who forgives all your sins. Leave vanity to the vain. Commit yourself to those things that God commands. Embrace solitude and spend much time with your beloved Jesus. Contemplation of Jesus affords a peace unattainable from any other source.

1 Discipline liberates. For most people, the word "discipline" elicits negative connotations. Only those, however, who practice playing the piano can make music through that instrument. If you do not subject yourself to the discipline of practice, you have no means to free the music within. The purpose of the practice is to free what you feel or know deep inside. Spiritual practices function in exactly the same way. Rather than being a burden—although discipline can be difficult at times—spiritual practices provide means to set the music of our real life free, liberating the true self to live from the resources of God.

2 Spiritual practices have a positive effect that moves in two directions simultaneously. Practice dismantles destructive patterns and rhythms that damage our lives; practice constructs virtues and dispositions that give life meaning, value, and purpose. We must unlearn and unsettle bad habits in order to construct new life-giving patterns that resituate us in God's way.

3 Thomas stresses the urgent nature of spiritual matters. Time is short and the task is large. Nothing should take priority over the cultivation of the spirit. He exhorts the reader to put first things first and to embark on an adventurous journey into God's love. Distractions make us go astray.

CHAPTER 13

☐ Discipline

If you want to make progress in your spiritual life, live in the awe of God (Proverbs 19:23). Do not seek too much freedom, submit yourself to the discipline of spiritual practices, and shun superficial and silly diversions.[1]

A proper attitude of deep respect for the Lord liberates the soul, producing both a joyful spirit and a good conscience. Blessed are you if you transcend those barriers that separate you from God. Blessed are you if true self-knowledge leads to contrition and repentance. Blessed are you if you resist behavior that pollutes the soul and burdens the conscience. Spiritual discipline overcomes bad habits and builds character.[2]

Scrutinize your own life, therefore, before you criticize others. Rather than obsessing over what others think about you, seek to live and act righteously as a true servant of God.... Nothing will make you more zealous for the things of God than seriously considering your own mortality instead of pursuing the comforts and joys of a long life. Wouldn't you endure any task, or sorrow, or sacrifice to avoid the pain of eternal separation from God? But if you refuse to let these concerns penetrate your heart—if the things of this world preoccupy your thoughts and dreams—then you will remain cold and lazy. You will be miserable, no matter where you are or where you go, unless you turn to God.... Dear friend, do not give up hope in the pursuit of spiritual things. There is yet time; your time is not yet past (Romans 13:11). Why wait any longer? Arise! Embrace your journey and say, "Now is the time to act, now is the time to fight, now is the time to improve my spiritual life."[3]

1 Contemplating our own mortality shocks us. It is so easy to get entangled in the things of this world, all of which are transitory diversions from the real thing. While Thomas's words have a morbid quality, they are meant to redirect our energies toward what really matters in life. It is hardly pleasant to consider the brevity and fragility of life, but a proper perspective on eternity and mortality keeps us oriented in a direction that leads to a deep sense of meaning, purpose, and value.

2 Having reminded the reader of the reality of death, Thomas turns his attention to the splendor of life. "I came that they may have life," Jesus claimed, "and have it abundantly" (John 10:10). Abundant life entails deep peace, overflowing gratitude, joyful security, healthy relationships, and an abiding sense of well-being. Whenever we live as God intended—when we enjoy life abundant in Jesus—we also experience eternal moments in the never-ending flow of time.

3 The world in which Thomas lived was much more precarious than our own. The cloud of death hovered over life as an ever-present specter. During the fourteenth century, for example, the Black Death decimated the European population, killing as many as one out of every two people. Despite the fact that improved standards of living and advances in health care cloak the reality of death for many today, tragedy wrenches us out of our complacency and illusion.

CHAPTER 14

☐ Mortality

This life will soon be at an end (Job 9:25–26).**1** Consider your status, therefore, with regard to eternity. You are here today and gone the next. Once you are out of sight you will soon be forgotten. So you should live each day, thinking and acting as if you were to die at any time (Matthew 25:13).... If you are not prepared today, how will you be ready tomorrow (Matthew 24:44)? Tomorrow is uncertain, and how do you know that you will even see it come?

What good is it to live a long life if you make no effort to improve it? A long life does not necessarily benefit you. On the contrary, it might just as easily add to your dis-ease. Would it not be sheer joy to live just one day in this world really well!**2**

When you wake up in the morning, consider the fact that you may die before the sun sets. When evening comes, do not promise yourself the next morning. Always be ready. Live in such a way that you are always prepared to die (Luke 21:36). Many die suddenly and unexpectedly.**3** "Therefore you also must be ready, for the Son of Man is coming at an unexpected hour" (Matthew 24:44). When that time comes, undoubtedly you will have a far different viewpoint with regard to your whole life.

Most certainly, you will be wise and happy if you try to live in this life the way you would wish to be found at the time of your death. While you are healthy you can do much good. When you are sick, however, you may have no strength to do anything.

(continued on page 35)

4 | Thomas continues to drive home these harsh realities. Distractions keep us from the intentional care of our souls.

5 | Life is precious. Thomas pleads for all to embrace the gift of life and to nurture dispositions that transcend death—virtues like faith, hope, and love. The only roadblocks to life with God are those we intentionally choose to put in the way. But if we keep our path open, faith, hope, and love can arise from the ordinary events of any day.

6 | Whatever you love becomes your God. You carry this God in your heart at all times. Thomas wants to make sure you know the one, true God and that this God alone fills your heart.

7 | Love is the source and the goal of the spiritual life. God manifests love in concrete ways through relationships. The primary goal of life is the fullest possible love of God and the fullest possible love of all others.

Do not put your trust in friends and family. Do not put off the care of your soul to some later time that may never come. Even your friends will forget you sooner than you would imagine.[4] If you are not concerned about your spiritual well-being now, who will care when you are gone? The present moment is very precious.[5] "See, now is the acceptable time; see, now is the day of salvation!" (2 Corinthians 6:2). How sad if you do not use the present time you are given to draw close to God. The time might come when you wish you had just one more day, one more hour, and you may just not have it.

Do now, my beloved, whatsoever you are able to do, for you do not know when death will come. While you have time, "store up for yourselves treasures in heaven, where neither moth nor rust consumes and where thieves do not break in and steal. For where your treasure is, there your heart will be also" (Matthew 6:20–21).[6] Above all things, consider the salvation of your soul. Focus your energy on the things of God.... Keep your heart free and lifted up to God, because love is the only thing that lasts.[7] Pray daily, with sighs and tears, that in death your spirit may happily pass to the Lord. Amen.

1 In his monumental treatise on the atoning work of Jesus, *Cur Deus Homo (Why God Became Human)*, St. Anselm (1033–1109), famed archbishop of Canterbury and medieval theologian, argues that most people do not give due consideration to the heavy weight of sin. But the consequences of sin are dire. The Psalmist understood the weight of sin when he confessed: "For my iniquities have gone over my head; they weigh like a burden too heavy for me" (Psalm 38:4).

2 "It is a fearful thing," claims the writer to the Hebrews, "to fall into the hands of the living God" (10:31). Martin Luther observed that if we tremble when we stand before an earthly king, how much more should we tremble before the Almighty God to whom all hearts are open and from whom no secrets are hid?

3 Psalm 139 opens with these penetrating words: "O Lord, you have searched me and known me" (1). A spiritual mentor told me that praying this Psalm every day for a month would change my life. Thomas awakens the reader to the same reality concerning God's knowledge of us.

4 In the concluding stanza of *And can it be that I should gain*, composed by Methodist hymn writer Charles Wesley (1707–1788), the singer proclaims: "No condemnation now I dread; Jesus, and all in Him, is mine! Alive in Him, my living Head, And clothed in righteousness divine, Bold I approach th'eternal throne, And claim the crown, through Christ my own."

CHAPTER 15

☐ The Consequences of Sin

In everything you do, consider the ultimate consequences.[1] Are your actions such that you could stand before a judge, from whom nothing is hid, with a clean conscience (Hebrews 10:31)?[2] God cannot be pacified with a bribe and will not be moved by your excuses, but judges on the sole basis of what is right. O wretched and foolish sinner. It is hard for you to even face the wrath of a person who is angry with you. What kind of defense do you think you can muster before the God who knows all your sins (Job 9:2)? Truly, on the great day of judgment there will be no more room for excuses or arguments, for all people will be called to give an account of themselves.

Search your heart now,[3] therefore, and repent of your sins so that you might be found among the righteous and enter into rest on that great and awful day. Justice will triumph in the end and the righteous will stand without fear before those who have abused and oppressed them. On that day, those who humbly submitted themselves to the judgment of others in this life will mete out justice on others. The poor and humble will stand confidently before God. On that day, God will scatter the proud in the thoughts of their hearts. God will bring down the powerful from their thrones and lift up the lowly (Luke 2:51–52).

Loving and serving God is the only thing that matters. If you love God with all your heart, then you need have no fear of death, or judgment, or hell.[4] Perfect love gives secure access to God (Romans 8:39).

1 Thomas returns to the journey motif. The path to spiritual maturity challenges each person in a way that is aligned with his or her own personality, areas of brokenness, and needs. While there may be remarkable similarities in the landscape of a pilgrimage, each person treads her or his own path.

2 When it comes to our movement toward God, all is grace. Thomas reminds us that "[f]rom his fullness we have all received, grace upon grace" (John 1:16). God graciously gives to us every spiritual gift that we need to progress on our way into the fullness of God's love. Those who remain focused and steadfast receive one blessing upon another, immeasurable grace and love.

3 We are not alone in our spiritual pilgrimage. Many have made this journey before us, and we can learn from them.

4 Keeping the eye of the soul fixed on Jesus is the key to faithfulness.

5 Jesus is not so much a master in the sense of someone who rules over us—although his rule in life is of singular importance—rather, he is a mentor who guides, challenges, encourages, and accompanies us. Jesus is our "companion"—the One who shares his bread with us on the journey—and if we imitate his way, we will certainly make it to journey's end.

CHAPTER 16

☐ Transformation

"Trust in the Lord, and do good," proclaims the prophet, "so you will live in the land, and enjoy security" (Psalm 37:3). Do not let your fear of the difficulty, or your concern about the energy it will require, dissuade you from the path that leads to spiritual growth.[1] You will develop a virtuous character if you seek to overcome those vices that are contrary to them. If you master yourself through the practice of spiritual disciplines, you will improve and grow from grace to grace (John 1:16).[2]

Make the best of every opportunity to cultivate your soul. If you see or hear of any good exemplars in the faith, study them closely and imitate what you see....[3] Never forget the important commitments you have made and keep the example of Jesus crucified ever before you. If you fix your attention on Jesus and seek to imitate him, the light of his grace will illuminate your shortcomings and reveal your weaknesses, even if you have made substantial progress in the spiritual life.[4] If you seek to follow Jesus and to imitate the holy life and passion of the Crucified you will discover everything necessary and profitable for your own growth in him. You will find no better master and guide than Jesus.[5] When you invite Jesus crucified into your heart, he will quickly and fully instruct you in all truth!

BOOK II
The Interior Life

1 Thomas advocates a religion of the heart. What happens inside us—in our hearts—is as important as our external actions. Those who seek to cultivate an interior life seek God in everything. They practice a life of prayer and live in the perennial presence of God. The interior life implies intimate conversation with God. External action (like an act of compassion) remains a vital part of an interior spirituality, because such actions are transformed into acts of prayer.

2 Scriptural images and metaphors dominate Thomas's description of the interior life, the primary characteristic of which is intimacy. Marriage often provides the most effective images for explaining spiritual matters in the Bible. The nuptial image of the bridegroom figures prominently in the writings of the Hebrew prophets, such as Hosea, Jeremiah, and Isaiah, and is exploited by St. Paul in Romans 5. More than anything else, this image stresses intimate, joyful, and fruitful union. God seeks this kind of intimacy with each of God's beloved children.

3 This language implies a kataphatic, or "affirming" spirituality, that is an approach to the spiritual life that emphasizes filling and the positive qualities of the Divine. Sometimes described as the "positive way," this path focuses on an intimate, tangible, and relational experience of God. If the self must be emptied (the apophatic way), the emptying is for the purpose of filling it with God.

4 This is a pervasive theme in Christian spirituality.

CHAPTER 1

☐ The Interior Life

"The kingdom of God is within you," says the Lord (Luke 17:21 King James Version). Turn with your whole heart to the Lord and abandon the temporary attractions of this world, and "you will find rest for your souls" (Matthew 11:29). Put superficial things in their proper place and devote yourself to the cultivation of an interior life, and you will see the reign of God come to you.[1] "For the kingdom of God is ... peace and joy in the Holy Spirit" (Romans 14:17).

Faithful soul, prepare your heart for the bridegroom that he may come and dwell within you![2] For Jesus has said, "Those who love me will keep my word, and my Father will love them, and we will come to them and make our home with them" (John 14:23). Open your heart to Jesus, therefore, and safeguard this sacred space for him alone. When you have Jesus, you are rich, and he alone will suffice.... "I am with you always," he promises, "to the end of the age" (Matthew 28:20).

Put your whole trust in God. Love God and let God's awesome nature fill you.[3] God will defend you, and do what is best for you all the time. You have no lasting place in this world. You are a stranger and pilgrim here (1 Peter 2:11).[4] You will have no rest until you are wholly united with Christ.

(continued on page 45)

43

5 Thomas stands in a medieval tradition that encouraged devotion to the five holy or sacred piercing wounds that Jesus suffered during the crucifixion. The image of "flying to the wounds," however, may be of Thomas's own creation. Bernard of Clairvaux and Francis of Assisi both advocated meditation on Jesus's wounds. The Jerusalem or Crusaders' Cross is comprised of five crosses for the five wounds. Many medieval prayers honored the wounds as well. Jesus's wounds from the crucifixion simply remind believers of the extent to which God's love will go to redeem and restore fallen humanity—to redeem each of us.

6 Jesus lived in solidarity with his human companions and experienced all the vicissitudes of life in this world, including the betrayal by those he loved. He suffers as we suffer. Our solidarity with him in suffering, however, can become a path to perfect freedom as long as it is all for the sake of love. Moreover, our identification with his suffering leads us to Christ in the world. Mother Teresa, laying a dying infant in the arms of my friend, asked, "Can you not see Christ in the face of this beloved child?" This elicited both his compassion and his action.

7 The reign of God refers both to the active rule of God in a person's heart and in the world.

Everything in this world passes away, and that includes you.... Fix your thoughts on God, therefore, and pray to Jesus without ceasing (1 Thessalonians 5:17). If you find it difficult to contemplate the things of God, then direct your thoughts to the sacrificial suffering of Jesus and meditate on his holy wounds. For if you fly devoutly to the precious wounds of the Lord Jesus Christ,[5] you will experience great comfort in tribulation, endure the scorn of others, and bear the slander of your detractors.

Remember that Jesus was also despised and forsaken by his closest friends and followers (Matthew 16:21).[6] He chose not to lash out against rejection, affliction, and suffering. How can you complain? He had plenty of opponents, adversaries, and slanderers, and would you desire only friends and benefactors? Adversity in life proves the strength of your patience. If you wish to avoid suffering at all costs, how can you be the friend of Christ who desires the reign of God above all things?[7]

1 "Staying close" to God says more about us than it says about God. Thomas believed unequivocally that God is always near, closer to us than our breath. But we often create barriers to that connectedness. Thomas's admonition to stay close to God entails an intentional desire to reach out to God, to remain connected with God, and to oppose any impediment to intimacy with God.

2 The human conscience functions essentially to help us distinguish good from evil. Medieval theologians focused a lot of energy on this topic. Thomas stands in a tradition that views the conscience as a critical aspect of spirituality. Certainly, he examined his own conscience daily in an effort to orient all his actions toward the good. He devotes an entire chapter to the good conscience in the original *Imitation of Christ*; excerpted here on page 55.

3 It is difficult for people to entrust their lives to God. We want to have control of our own lives. We put our trust in ourselves, our things, our own efforts—in self-reliance. Thomas, in contrast, encourages trust in God, because he knew that God wholeheartedly desires only the best for us all and loves us even more than we love ourselves.

4 This could be called "God's preferential option for the humble." Humility, like all other aspects of the Christian faith, ultimately relates to trust.

CHAPTER 2

☐ Humble Submission

Do not be concerned about who is for you or who is against you. Stay close to God in everything you do.[1] Maintain a good conscience and God will defend you.[2] "If God is for us, who is against us?" (Romans 8:31). If you are able to maintain a spirit of peace in the midst of suffering, then you will see the salvation of the Lord. God knows when and how to deliver you, so resign yourself to God in all things.[3]

God protects and liberates, loves and consoles the humble. Great grace surrounds them. God lifts up the lowly (Luke 1:52). God reveals the deepest secrets to the humble and with kind invitation bids the meek to draw near. If you are humble—resting in God rather than putting your trust in the world—then no vexations will be too great for you and peace will be your constant companion.[4]

1 This statement resonates with other similar affirmations in scripture. "We love," for example, "because [God] first loved us" (1 John 4:19). We are only able to share with others what we have experienced or possess.

2 An interior disposition carries far more weight than an exterior qualification.

3 What sound advice! The images that follow all derive from Jesus's Sermon on the Mount: "Do not judge, so that you may not be judged. For with the judgment you make you will be judged, and the measure you give will be the measure you get. Why do you see the speck in your neighbor's eye, but do not notice the log in your own eye? Or how can you say to your neighbor, 'Let me take the speck out of your eye,' while the log is in your own eye? You hypocrite, first take the log out of your own eye, and then you will see clearly to take the speck out of your neighbor's eye" (Matthew 7:1–5).

4 The true test of goodness is the ability to love the unlovable. St. Francis of Assisi experienced a spiritual breakthrough in his life when he began to care for lepers who had been abandoned and marginalized in his community.

CHAPTER 3

☐ Peace and Goodness

If you have peace in your own heart, you will be able to offer peace to others.**1** You will do more good with your peace than with years of education.**2** When your passions dominate, you believe the worst about others and easily turn good into evil. But if peace reigns in your heart, you can turn everything into good. Peace removes all suspicion (1 Corinthians 13:5). When you are disturbed and discontented, you cannot quiet your inner self and cannot stand the peace you see in others. You say things you should not say and fail to do those things you know are right. "For I do not do the good I want," as St. Paul observes, "but the evil I do not want is what I do" (Romans 7:19).

Self-examination always ought to precede your judgment of others.**3** Be as zealous for your neighbor's good as you are for your own. You know how easy it is to excuse your own actions, so do not be quick to accuse others. Is it not more just to accuse yourself and excuse others? If you want others to bear with you, then cut others the same slack you cut yourself (Galatians 6:2).... It is no great accomplishment to live peaceably with good folk; everyone loves those who are easy to love, especially those who think and act as you do. But to be able to live in peace with harsh and unlovable people is another matter altogether. That is the true test of goodness.**4**

1 This is one of the most celebrated chapters of *The Imitation of Christ*. Read and re-read it often. Deeply ponder Thomas's counsel. He opens with a poignant image: Simplicity and purity are like two wings that enable the soul to soar. Simplicity of intention means that you have one aim or desire—your eye is fixed on one thing. Purity of desire means that you have no ulterior motive, no selfish goal.

2 In other words, if you love God simply for the sake of loving God, and love yourself and all else as means to love God more fully, then all the loving you do will be simple and pure. This concept derives primarily from St. Augustine.

3 Genuine love always has two directions: love of God and love of neighbor. As Jesus claimed, "There is no other commandment greater than these" (Mark 12:31).

4 Note the way in which Thomas consistently emphasizes interiority. Our internal condition determines how we interpret things on the outside.

5 Jesus says, "Blessed are the pure in heart, for they will see God" (Matthew 5:8).

6 The restoration of the image of God in the beloved creature is the goal of the spiritual life. Such change normally entails a lengthy process because of the vast chasm between what we ought to be inside and what we are. Ultimately, we cannot force ourselves to exhibit the qualities of simplicity and purity; rather, God shapes them within us as we apprentice ourselves to the master of these virtues. St. Athanasius (c. 296–373), the great champion of orthodoxy and bishop of Alexandria, maintained that Jesus became what we are in order that we might become what he is.

CHAPTER 4
☐ Simplicity and Purity

Twin wings elevate the human soul: simplicity of intention and purity of desire.[1] Simplicity leads to God; purity embraces and enjoys God forever. If your heart is free from disordered affections,[2] then putting your love into action will not be hard for you. If you intend and seek nothing but the will of God and the good of your neighbor,[3] you will be truly free. When your heart is in the right place, all creation functions like a mirror of life—a holy book that leads to God. No matter how small or seemingly insignificant, every creature points to the goodness of God. When you are good and pure, you see and understand all things from the right perspective. The condition of your inner self determines how you judge everything around you.[4] If there is any joy in this world, surely the pure in heart possess it.[5] On the other hand, an evil conscience knows tribulation and affliction all too well. Just as fire purifies iron—removing its rust so that it glows with radiant beauty—God will remove all your slothfulness and recreate you in God's own image if you desire God wholly with purity of intention.[6]

☩ In order to live life to the fullest, people must come to a proper self-understanding. In the account of the prodigal son, spiritual transformation began only "when he came to himself" (Luke 15:17). Authentic self-knowledge entails a paradoxical insight. First, we realize how far we have strayed from God's intention—proper self-understanding entails acknowledgment of one's fallen and broken condition. But secondly, we also realize that we are beloved children of God, and the discovery of this primary identity provides the only secure foundation for a life of love.

1 Spiritual health begins with serious introspection.

2 This pithy statement functions like a basic philosophy of life, and if followed, leads to peace, happiness, security, and joy.

3 Thomas returns to the Augustinian theme of properly ordered affections. The child of God, whose loves have been properly rearranged by God's grace, loves God for God's self and loves all others as a means to a more perfect love of God. The primary problem of human beings is their inordinate and misplaced love of self above all things.

CHAPTER 5

☐ Self-Understanding

Do not put too much trust in yourself (Jeremiah 17:5), because a lack of grace and understanding can easily pervert your judgment. Truth to be told, you only possess a little light and you lose quickly what you have through negligence. So small faults in others drive you crazy, but you ignore monumental problems in yourself. You overemphasize the harm done to you by others, but take little notice of the wounds you inflict. If you scrutinize your own actions with authenticity, you will find little cause to judge others harshly.

You will never be a truly religious person until you understand yourself more fully than you seek to understand others. If you focus your attention on God and yourself, you will not be distracted from whatever you see around you. Where are your thoughts when they are not on yourself? After you have surveyed everyone else's life, what has it profited you if you have neglected your own soul?[1] If you desire genuine peace of mind, you must keep self in your mind's eye at all times and not worry about other people.

Consider nothing great, hold nothing in high esteem, take pleasure in nothing other than God and that which comes from God.[2] Place little value on those momentary comforts and pleasures of this life. If you love God in the proper manner, you will love everything else for God's sake.[3] God alone—the eternal, awesome, and glorious One—will satisfy your deepest longings and radiate true joy throughout your heart.

1 Having introduced the concept of the conscience earlier, Thomas returns to this central theme and elaborates what he means by a good conscience.

2 The internal testimony of a clear conscience—the ability to look at oneself in the mirror—far outweighs the opinion of others.

3 Thomas identifies the most important aspects of life.

4 Note again the central importance of the interior life—the religion of the heart—in these statements. The influential African American preacher and Quaker mystic Howard Thurman (1899–1981) once observed that the heart is the citadel of all our human longings. The Negro spiritual proclaims, "Lord, I want to be a Christian, in my heart."

5 Humility must sit on the throne of the human heart.

CHAPTER 6

☐ A Good Conscience

The testimony of a good conscience is a glorious thing.[1] If your conscience is clear, you will always rejoice exceedingly; you will rest in peace if there is nothing in your heart to condemn you. A godly life leads to great joy, but sinners neither experience true joy nor feel inward peace, for "[t]here is no peace," says the Lord, "for the wicked" (Isaiah 48:22).

The glory of the godly rests in their good consciences and not in the praise of the people....[2] The level of praise you receive from others in this life measures neither your holiness nor your wickedness. You are not more holy because you are praised; neither are you more sinful if you are scorned. You are what you are. The most important thing is who you are in the sight of God.[3] If you have integrity and know who you are, then you will pay no attention to what others say about you. People see the face; God looks into the heart (1 Samuel 16:7). People consider the deeds, but God weighs the intention.[4] The true mark of humility is your desire to please God and to measure your life against God's standard.

Your desire for God—and God alone—to see your good deeds reflects total commitment to God. "For it is not those who commend themselves that are approved," says St. Paul, "but those whom the Lord commends" (2 Corinthians 10:18). The truly spiritual person walks humbly with God (Micah 6:8) and abides with God in the innermost part of their being.[5]

1 The title "Love of Jesus" reflects a double entendre. Does this phrase mean our love of Jesus or Jesus's love of us? The answer, of course, is "yes." Human love, however, depends completely on Jesus's love. His love is steadfast, unwavering—a commitment to us that death itself cannot destroy. Nothing in the universe is more dependable than the love of Jesus.

2 In contrast to the love of Jesus, all other loves are fragile and partial, even the love of those closest to us in life.

3 Thomas provides a natural segue to the following chapter. Jesus offers a precious gift in his friendship. One of the greatest British Methodist preachers, Leslie Weatherhead (1893–1976), described this relationship as a "transforming friendship." A vital relationship with this friend entails growth and change as one develops a greater capacity for love throughout life.

CHAPTER 7

☐ Love of Jesus

You are truly blessed if you understand (Psalm 119:1–2) what it means to love Jesus and to deny self for Jesus's sake. He desires for you to love him with your whole heart. The love of any object as an end in itself—whether a person or a thing—only leads to deceit and infidelity. The love of Jesus is faithful and constant. If you attach yourself inordinately to things and other persons, you will fall whenever they fall. If you embrace Jesus, you will stand firmly forever. Love him and maintain the closest of friendships with him. When others abandon you—as they will do inevitably—Jesus will never forsake you.[1]

If you entrust your life to other people, they will frequently disappoint and wound you. Do not lean on a fragile blade of grass. "All flesh is like grass and all its glory like the flower of grass. The grass withers, and the flower falls" (1 Peter 1:24).[2]

So do not depend on the outward appearances of those who seek your trust, for they will certainly deceive and disappoint you. If you seek comfort and gain through them, you will lose in the end. But if you seek Jesus in all things, you will surely find the best friend of your entire life.[3]

1 Thomas contrasts the presence and absence of Jesus in dramatic fashion. Lazarus, Mary, and Martha of Bethany were some of Jesus's closest friends. Thomas draws an important inference from the account of Jesus's raising of Lazarus from death in John's Gospel. Jesus's companionship offers life; life without Jesus signals death. When Jesus comes near and we accept his offer of friendship, all things are possible—he even has the power to transform death into life.

2 All relationships—all friendships—involve effort and intentionality. Whenever we "pour ourselves" into other people, that sustained action demonstrates our genuine concern and love for them. We cannot simply glide in relationships. Either we invest energy in them, or they die. Our friendship with Jesus is no different.

3 Permit nothing to take priority over your relationship with God.

CHAPTER 8

☐ Friendship with Jesus

When Jesus is present, all is well. But when Jesus is absent, everything is difficult. If you are unable to hear Jesus's voice within, you have no true comfort. But if you are attentive and Jesus speaks just one word, you experience great consolation. Did not Mary rise up from the place where she wept when Martha exclaimed, "The Teacher is here and is calling for you" (John 11:28)? Happy the hour when Jesus calls you from tears to spiritual joy. Without Jesus, you are dry and cold! You are foolish and vain if you desire anything other than Jesus! The loss of Jesus is far greater than losing the whole world (Matthew 16:26).[1]

If you are humble and peaceable, Jesus will be with you. If you are devout and still, Jesus will stay with you. You may drive Jesus out of your life if you constantly turn to worldly, superficial things. And if you drive him away, to whom will you go, and what friend will you seek?[2] Without a friend like Jesus, you can never live well. If Jesus is not the most important friend of your life, you will become sorrowful and inconsolable....[3] Of all the things that you cherish, therefore, love none more than you love Jesus. Love all things in Jesus, but love Jesus for himself. Jesus Christ alone is to be beloved. He alone is faithful above all friends. Embrace your friends and foes alike for the sake of Jesus, and pray for all of them that they may know and love Jesus as their friend as well.

Let no one come in the way of your friendship with Jesus.

1 Every good gift comes from God as a consequence of grace. Grace defines and shapes every aspect of life for the follower of Jesus.

2 Thomas uses an episode in the life of David the Psalmist to illustrate the reality and function of God's grace as well as the importance of God's presence. In Psalm 30 David expressed his gratitude to God for recovery. He experienced the absence of God after a period of blessing, and this disturbed him deeply. He was comfortless. But God reoriented David, moving him from a place of lament to a place of praise. God's grace functions in this way to bring comfort to all who are afflicted.

CHAPTER 9

☐ Divine Comfort

Whenever God comforts your heart, receive this gift with great thanksgiving for it is not something you have earned or achieved.[1] Do not be proud or presumptuous; rather, be all the more humble on account of the gift and all the more careful about your actions, for the temptation to put your trust elsewhere will quickly return.

When God's grace enveloped the life of David, the Israelite proclaimed, "As for me ... I shall never be moved." But in the absence of God's presence, having experienced who he was apart from God, the Psalmist adds, "you hid your face; I was dismayed." In his need, then, he prayed to the Lord all the more earnestly: "To you, O Lord, I cried, and to the Lord I made supplication." Only then did he receive the fruit of faithful prayer, bearing witness to the comfort of the Lord: "Hear, O Lord, and be gracious to me! O Lord, be my helper! You have turned my mourning into dancing; you have taken off my sackcloth and clothed me with joy" (Psalm 30:6–11).[2]

(continued on page 63)

3 ┃ Thomas returns to the theme of trust or faith. That to which we entrust our lives becomes our god. The one, true God upon whom we can always depend is the God of grace and mercy known in Jesus.

4 ┃ Spiritual comfort depends ultimately on the disposition of the will. Peace comes when conflict no longer exists between our deepest desires and the longings of the Spirit of God.

5 ┃ The desire to stand alone, autonomous and unconnected to any other, diminishes the capacity to love. Genuine love entails relationship; relationships fuel authentic love. All human misery emanates from an autonomous posture in life. St. Augustine located the source of all pride in this desire to be like God—in this conviction that "I" stand alone and need no other.

In what can you hope, then—in what can you put your trust with absolute certainty—the great mercy and grace of God and that alone![3] If you surround yourself with good people, devout companions, faithful friends, holy and incisive books, sweet songs and hymns, all these things provide little solace if you cannot connect with God's grace and are left to face your own inadequacies apart from God. At such times, the only way to find divine comfort is to remain patient and to pray for the ability to align your will with the will of God.[4]

God comforts those in tribulation in order to help them bear the adversities of life. In such situations, however, pride often follows, with its temptation to seduce you into thinking that you can make it on your own.[5] Beware of this subtle tempter who lurks in the midst of your consolation. Always be prepared to battle your pride, for it stands to your left and your right as a perennial enemy that never rests.

✠ The terms "grace" and "gratitude" come from the same root. Given the fact that everything comes from God as a consequence of grace, those with a proper attitude respond with gratitude or thanks. Gratitude is the disposition; thanks is the action. Those who live by grace (*charis*), respond with thanksgiving (*eucharistia*). Those who follow the way of Jesus cultivate this disposition through practice— they practice giving thanks—and the Spirit of God shapes the faithful "eucharistically" through action.

1 Note the intimate connections between grace, gratitude, thanksgiving, and humility. The dispositions of gratitude and humility go hand in hand. You cannot express gratitude to yourself! Your gratitude reflects your understanding that relationships define who you are. Gratitude only happens in relationship to others. Appreciation for others sows the seed of humility in your life.

2 This banquet story provides a potent narrative illustration of the interconnected nature of humility and gratitude.

3 Thomas does not believe that grace is irresistible; it is relational. Since grace is a gift it can be either accepted or rejected. It can be lost as well as embraced, and only the humble retain the most important gifts of God.

CHAPTER 10

☐ Gratitude

Nothing brings greater joy to God than showering grace on everything and everyone. The only proper response to this lavish gift is the grateful return of all to God. The gifts of grace cannot flow in you if you show no gratitude to the Giver. Grace and gratitude spring from the same root. Those who are thankful abide in grace; God brings down the proud and elevates the humble. Not all that is high is holy, nor is all that is sweet good, nor every desire pure, nor is everything dear to you pleasing to God. Open your heart to that grace which leads to humility and a healthy renunciation of self....[1] Give to God what is God's and ascribe to yourself what is yours. Express your gratitude to God for the gift of grace; acknowledge that you have nothing to offer except your own sinfulness and poverty of spirit.

"Go and sit down at the lowest place," says Jesus, "so that when your host comes, he may say to you, 'Friend, move up higher;' then you will be honored in the presence of all who sit at the table with you. For all who exalt themselves will be humbled, and those who humble themselves will be exalted" (Luke 14:10–11).[2] The saints who are the greatest before God are those who consider themselves to be the least; the greater the humility, the greater the glory in God's realm. If you are rooted and grounded in God, there is no way you can be proud.

If you want to stay in love with God, be thankful for every gift from God's hand and patiently await God's mercy. Pray for grace and retain it in humility.[3]

1 These opening statements sear the conscience. They cut to the quick. Dietrich Bonhoeffer (1906–1945), the Lutheran theologian martyred for his resistance to Nazi oppression, talked frequently about the cost of discipleship. To be a true follower of Jesus means to take up a cross and to die. Those who seek to imitate Christ must be willing to suffer and die with him.

2 Teresa of Avila (1515–1582), the sixteenth-century Carmelite reformer and author of *The Interior Castle*, suffered deep depression for as many as thirteen years, but retained her trust in God through some of the darkest moments.

3 William Temple (1881–1944), archbishop of Canterbury during the Second World War, coined the term "disinterested love" as a modern English rendering of the *agape*—self-sacrificing love—of Jesus. By this term he meant a love that has no self-interest attached to it. This highest form of love never asks the question "What is in this for me?" It gives without counting the cost and is willing to give all for the sake of the other. As the writer of John's Gospel claims: "No one has greater love than this, to lay down one's life for one's friends" (John 15:13).

CHAPTER 11

☐ The Cross of Christ

Jesus has many lovers of his heavenly realm, but few bearers of his cross. He has many who seek the comfort only he can give, but few who embrace his suffering. He finds many companions at his table, but few who are willing to share his discipline of fasting. All want a part of his happiness, but few want to suffer anything for his sake.[1] Many love Jesus as long as they encounter no hardships in life. Many praise and bless him as long as they enjoy the comforts of a good life. But if Jesus hides himself, even for a moment, they immediately begin to complain and feel dejected.

But those who truly love Jesus for Jesus's sake, and not for what they can get out of him, bless him at all times, both when they are devastated with broken hearts and when they are filled with ecstatic joy. Even if Jesus were never to give them comfort again, they would praise him forever and always give him thanks.[2]

Oh, how powerful is the pure love of Jesus, mixed with no self-love or self-interest![3]

1 According to Thomas, life in this world must always be kept in proper perspective. Some of the decisions we make in this life have eternal consequences.

2 Thomas identifies here some of the facets of the journey or way of the cross. This itemized list provides a vision of dignity—life lived at this most lofty level.

3 Historians of Christian doctrine describe the theology of Martin Luther (1483–1546), the sixteenth-century Christian reformer and father of Protestantism, as a theology of the cross. Everything in his theology revolves around the cross of Jesus. The cross provides the interpretive key for everything from human redemption to the purpose of the universe. For Thomas, the cross functions in very much the same way.

4 The follower of Jesus conforms his or her life to the shape of the cross. Jesus extends his arms on the hard wood of the cross to take the whole world into his loving embrace. The Christian disciple imitates this posture in life.

CHAPTER 12

☐ The Royal Way

Jesus's words may sound harsh to many: "If any want to become my followers, let them deny themselves and take up their cross and follow me" (Matthew 16:24). Is it not much more harsh, however, to hear the final words, "Depart from me into the eternal fire" (Matthew 25:41)? The sign of the cross will fill the heavens when our Lord comes in final judgment. At that time, all those who have been servants of the cross will draw near to Christ the Judge with great confidence.[1]

Why do you fear, therefore, to take up your cross, which epitomizes Jesus's reign? Salvation comes through the cross. The cross offers life. It protects you against all evil. Heavenly sweetness, strength of mind, joy of spirit, height of virtue, and perfection in holiness characterize the way of the cross.[2] There is no salvation of the soul, nor hope of everlasting life, apart from the cross.[3] Take up your cross, therefore, and follow Jesus (Luke 14:27), and you will enjoy eternal life. Jesus has gone before, bearing his cross (John 19:17), and died for you there that you might also bear your cross and die with him there.[4] "If we have died with Christ," so St. Paul proclaims, "we believe that we will also live with him" (Romans 6:8). If you have shared his pain, you will also share his glory.

(continued on page 71)

69

5   If the cross becomes the lens through which you interpret life, then you will find the cross in everything.

6   The self-sacrificial love of Jesus was not new in the crucifixion; such love has always been in the heart of God. The faithful of every age have taken on the "posture of the cruciform life." The Psalmist proclaims: "Because of you we are being killed all day long, and accounted as sheep for the slaughter" (Psalm 44:22). In this world, to stand on the side of justice and love often leads to death.

7   The "royal way" implies the highest road, the way of the king, the path that leads to the dominion of God. Those who seek to be co-heirs with Christ are invited to follow this path. The primary requirement for those who travel the way of Jesus is a commitment to self-sacrificing love. This road may lead to a cross, but the resurrection awaits those who live in solidarity with all who suffer. In the reign of God death always gives way to life.

No matter which way you turn—look up and down, inside yourself and all around you—you will encounter the cross.[5] Everything, therefore, demands your patience, if you desire an everlasting crown.... So embrace your calling as a faithful servant of Jesus and bear the cross of your Lord with courage and steadfast love. This is no easy task! Many obstacles and barriers will clutter your path. But drink the cup of the Lord gladly (Matthew 20:23), if you want to be his friend. Leave the comforts to God. Let God handle things as seems best for you. Certainly, prepare to suffer and consider even these painful moments as comforts in your journey with Jesus, for what you endure in this life is not even worth comparing to the glory which is to come.

Know for certain that you are called to lead a dying life—a life conformed to the self-sacrificing actions of the cross (Psalm 44:22).[6] The more you die to yourself, the more you live to God.... So Jesus plainly exhorts all God's children to live cruciform lives, saying, "If any want to become my followers, let them deny themselves and take up their cross daily and follow me" (Luke 9:23). When you have read everything and pursued every avenue to find the way to abundant life, let this be your final conclusion—it is through the royal way of the cross[7] that we enter the kingdom of God.

BOOK III
The Comfort of the Heart

1 Thomas changes his style of presentation in Book III and moves into a dialogical format. "The Disciple" enters into a conversation with "Christ."

2 This opening paragraph is reminiscent of the Beatitudes in Jesus's Sermon on the Mount in Matthew 5. The primary image relates to listening and responding faithfully to the voice of God. God's speech is a source of comfort, truth, and wisdom.

3 In order to hear the voice of God, it is necessary to shut out the noises of the world and the clamor of voices within that compete for our attention. Note that we listen with our hearts and not with our ears.

4 Christ describes himself clearly to those who are attentive to his voice. His opening words in the dialogue provide a roadmap to happiness—to blessedness in life.

5 This is not a message we want to hear. We like to live in the illusion that things give us security. But God is the only source of peace; everything else will pass away. True security rests in a heart truly aligned with God's will and way.

CHAPTER 1

☐ Christ Speaks

THE VOICE OF THE DISCIPLE:**1** I will listen to the words the Lord God speaks to my heart (Psalm 85:8). Blessed is the soul that hears the Lord speaking, who receives comfort from the words of God's mouth.**2** Blessed are those ears that hear the whispers of the divine voice (Matthew 13:16–17) and turn a deaf ear to the seductive clamor of the world. Blessed indeed are those ears that shut out the worldly cacophony of sound, but attend to the still small voice within that teaches truth. Blessed are the eyes that are shut to outward appearances, but remain open to internal, spiritual impressions. Blessed are those who delight to abide in God and purge themselves of worldly diversions.

Consider these things, my soul, and close the door of your sensual desires, that you may hear the voice of the Lord in your heart.**3**

THE VOICE OF CHRIST: I am your peace, your life, and your salvation (Psalm 35:3).**4** Stay close to me and you will find peace. Abandon the things of this world and seek those things that last forever. The trifles of this world are only snares. And what good are other people if you are forsaken by the Creator? Forsake all earthly things, therefore, and seek to please the Lord.**5** Put your trust in God if you want to find true happiness.

1 The words of scripture constitute the internal voice of the believer. The disciple fills his or her heart with the wisdom of the Hebrew Bible, all condensed in one word: listen. Faithfulness begins with the desire to listen to God.

2 The faithful disciple stands with Samuel over those who trust in things rather than God. While the Israelites' account of the giving of the Law in the Exodus feared the voice of God, Samuel welcomes it, engages God in conversation, and seeks to respond to God's call faithfully. God calls; Samuel answers. God's voice captures his attention, and he has no desire to hear any other voice once he has heard from God.

3 In a series of potent parallel statements, Thomas describes the monumental distinction between God's voice and the voice of all others. Profound oratory and persuasive arguments may have compelling elements, but nothing compares to the voice of God. The question is: To whom do you listen?

CHAPTER 2

☐ The Internal Voice

THE VOICE OF THE DISCIPLE: "Speak, Lord, for your servant is listening" (1 Samuel 3:9). "I am your servant; give me understanding, so that I may know your decrees" (Psalm 119:125). "Turn my heart to your decrees" (Psalm 119:36). "May [your] speech condense like the dew" (Deuteronomy 32:2). The children of Israel said unto Moses, "You speak to us, and we will listen; but do not let God speak to us, or we will die" (Exodus 20:19).[1]

Not so, Lord, not so, I beg you; rather, with the prophet, Samuel, I humbly and earnestly implore you, "Speak, Lord, for your servant is listening."[2] I do not want Moses to speak to me, or any of the prophets. I want you to speak, O God, for you are the One who inspired and enlightened all the prophets. Only you can instruct me perfectly. Their words mean nothing to me apart from you.

They may speak boldly, but they cannot fill me with your spirit. They speak well, but if you are silent, nothing inspires my heart. They teach the letter, but you reveal the true sense. They describe mysteries, but you unlock their meaning. They declare your commandments, but you empower me to fulfill them. They show the way, but you provide strength to walk in it. They work on the externals, but you instruct and enlighten the heart. They water, but only you can give the growth (1 Corinthians 3:7). They make a noise with words, but you give the understanding.[3]

Speak, Lord, for your servant is listening. You have the words of eternal life (John 6:68).

1 Christ initiates the dialogue in this chapter. The disciple assumes a posture of humility and listens attentively in love.

2 The disciple responds with the words of the Psalmist.

3 God speaks in the "language of promise." Martin Luther defined his theology in relation to God's promises: the supply of our needs, victory over death, eternal life, and many other amazing gifts. In his view, God always complements our faith with a glorious promise.

4 Thomas uses a profound scriptural image. We are called to write God's words on our hearts. "I will put my law within them," says the Lord, "and I will write it on their hearts; and I will be their God, and they shall be my people" (Jeremiah 31:33). Some people inscribe God's Word on their hearts by committing scripture to memory. This is one of the ways we make God's words our own. Held in the heart in this way, God's words serve to comfort and encourage in times of difficulty and despair.

5 These stark contrasts between the Creator and the creature emphasize God's transcendence. In the face of such a "tremendous Majesty," it is normal to feel overwhelmed—even to feel like nothing.

6 The transcendent nature of God does not repel Thomas; rather, he turns immediately toward God in prayer.

CHAPTER 3

☐ God's Word

THE VOICE OF CHRIST:**1** My beloved, hear my words, words of the greatest sweetness, excelling all the knowledge of the philosophers and the wise of this world. "The words that I have spoken to you are spirit and life" (John 6:63). They cannot be measured by the wisdom of this age. Listen to my words in silence; receive them with humility and great affection.

THE VOICE OF THE DISCIPLE: "Happy are those whom you discipline, O Lord, and whom you teach out of your law, giving them respite from days of trouble" (Psalm 94:12–13).**2**

THE VOICE OF CHRIST: I will give all I have promised and will fulfill all I have said to those who remain faithful in my love to the end....**3** Write my words in your heart,**4** and meditate on them earnestly, for they will help you greatly in times of temptation. Those things you find difficult to understand in my Word, you will comprehend fully in the time to come.

THE VOICE OF THE DISCIPLE: O Lord my God, you are good all the time. Who am I even to speak to you? I am your lowest servant—so impotent and contemptible. You know, O Lord, that I am nothing, have nothing, and can do nothing. You alone are good, just, and holy. You can do all things. You fill all things.**5** But you send the proud away empty (Luke 1:53). Be merciful to me and fill my heart with your grace.... Lord, teach me to fulfill your will and to live worthily and humbly in your sight. For you are my wisdom. You know me through and through. You called me before I was born, while I was in my mother's womb you named me (Isaiah 49:1).**6**

1 Keynotes of authentic Christianity include liberty and integrity. God seeks freedom for all, and the primary purpose of all spiritual practices is liberation. We imitate Christ in order to liberate the true self, often broken, in bondage, or hidden deep inside.

2 Spiritual health and vitality begin with the acknowledgment of our brokenness and our need for help.

3 This seems to be a harsh analysis of the human situation. But Thomas is convinced that our pride and our tendency to place self at the center of all we are and do separate us from God. Sin turns us away from our greatest good. More often than not, we need to be shocked out of our complacency and false sense of self-importance.

4 Three qualities together characterize the authentic disciple: an enlightened mind, a purified heart, and a focused desire to please God.

5 Thomas continues to explore the importance of the interior life. We get caught up so easily in the "externals" and thereby miss the real thing—the life of God in the soul of God's creatures. Henry Scougal (1650–1678), a Scottish theologian and spiritual writer, described authentic Christianity in this kind of language. "Heart religion" is the only true religion.

CHAPTER 4

☐ Truth and Humility

THE VOICE OF CHRIST: My beloved, walk before me in truth and always seek me in simplicity of heart, for I will defend all who seek integrity and authenticity. My truth will liberate you from all those forces that seek to lead you astray. "So if the Truth makes you free, you will be free indeed" (John 8:36).**1**

THE VOICE OF THE DISCIPLE: Lord, your words are truth and life to me. Teach me your ways, keep me, and bring me in safety to a happy end.

THE VOICE OF CHRIST: I will teach you those things that are right and pleasing in my sight. First of all, repent of your sins and take no pride in your good works.**2** You are a sinner.... Nothing that you do is great, precious, or wonderful. Do not value your deeds more highly than you ought; nothing you do is truly noble, high, or praiseworthy.**3** Above all things, revel in God's eternal truth.

Some believe that religion consists primarily of books, others of images, still others of outward forms and ceremonies. Some "draw near with their mouths and honor me with their lips, while their hearts are far from me" (Isaiah 29:13). There are authentic disciples, however, whose minds have been illumined, whose hearts have been purged of inordinate affections, and who pant now after the form of true godliness.**4** These perceive what the Spirit of truth speaks in them. It teaches them to despise earthly and to love heavenly things, to abandon this world and yearn for heaven all the daylong and throughout the night.**5**

1 The thought of God's love elicits a prayer of thanksgiving and adoration. Thomas concludes his prayer with a threefold petition—a poignant expression of his primary needs as he perceives them.

2 Christ responds to Thomas's prayer with a definitive statement about God's love, similar to the portrait painted by St. Paul in his famous "love chapter" (1 Corinthians 13). Note the many nouns he uses to describe love, but look even more closely at the verbs. Love ightens, relieves, and bears; it inspires and stirs up; it soars, flies, runs, leaps, and transcends. Thomas conceives love as an active force, not something passive or dormant. God puts love into action, and that active energy elevates the soul.

CHAPTER 5

☐ Divine Love

THE VOICE OF THE DISCIPLE: I praise you, O God, Father of my Lord Jesus Christ, for you have promised to remember me, your humble child.... I will always bless and glorify you, with your only begotten Son, and the Holy Spirit, forever and ever. O God, the holy lover of my soul, whenever you come into my heart, all that is within me rejoices. You are my glory and the joy of my heart. "For you have been a fortress for me and a refuge in the day of my distress" (Psalm 59:16).... Make me fit to love, strong to suffer, and constant to persevere.[1]

THE VOICE OF CHRIST: Love is a mighty power, a great and complete good. Love alone lightens every burden, and relieves all uneasiness. It bears every hardship as though it was nothing, and renders all bitterness sweet and acceptable. It inspires great action and stirs up the desire for even deeper love. Love soars and cannot be held down.... Nothing is sweeter than love, nothing stronger, nothing higher, nothing wider, nothing more pleasant, nothing fuller or better in heaven or earth, "because love is from God" (1 John 4:7). Love flies, runs, and leaps for joy. It is free and unrestrained. Love knows no limits; it transcends all boundaries.[2]

(continued on page 85)

3 These images emphasize the limitless nature of God's love. Such a love cannot be exhausted. It exceeds all expectations. In the Christian heritage, fire often symbolizes love, a most potent image signifying this boundless quality. About a century before the time of Thomas, the great English mystic Richard Rolle (1290–1349) published a classic text entitled the *Fire of Love*. He describes encounter with God in three stages: We experience God's love, first, as the glowing presence of a fire that brings physical warmth. The fire swells, leading to peace and joy. Finally, the seeker unites with God, becoming one with the flame of love.

4 The practical mysticism of Thomas shines through in this statement. In union with God, love provides the means of communion.

5 Having listened to Christ's description of love, Thomas breaks into prayer once again, seemingly overwhelmed by the power of the images. The reality of God's love evokes a deep yearning, expressed in yet another set of poignant images about this love: to melt in it, to swim in it, to taste its sweetness. The heart engulfed with this love not only loves fully, but loves properly.

Love feels no burden, takes no account of hardship, exceeds its own apparent strength. Love knows no impossibilities; "for God all things are possible" (Mark10:27). It is effective and sustaining; those who lack love faint and fail.... Love is not fickle and sentimental, nor is it superficial. Like a living flame and a burning torch, it surges upward and surmounts every obstacle....[3] The loving soul cries out, "My God, my love, you are all mine, and I am all yours."[4]

THE VOICE OF THE DISCIPLE: Increase this love in me, that in my innermost being I may taste the sweetness of your love. Melt my heart that I may swim in your love.... Let me sing the song of love and follow you into the heavens, my beloved. Let my soul soar in your praise and rejoice in your love. Let me love you more than myself, and love myself only in you. Let me love all things in you as your law of love commands.[5]

1 Grace relates to God's offer of love to people whether they deserve it or not. This grace is a free gift, offered to all. So God's free grace means the most to those who feel furthest from God. In the face of God's awe and majesty, the genuinely humble child of God experiences God's unconditional love as something equal and opposite to his or her own sense of depravity.

2 In some theological traditions, this is known as "prevenient grace"— that grace which comes before everything else. Our whole existence is enveloped by the wooing activity of God's grace.

3 Thomas refers to a great spiritual paradox. As Jesus maintained: "For those who want to save their life will lose it, and those who lose their life for my sake will find it" (Matthew 16:25).

4 God's love extends to every person in every place in every time.

5 In typical fashion, overwhelmed by the thought of God's unconditional love, the disciple turns to prayer and expresses gratitude to God.

CHAPTER 6

☐ Free Grace

THE VOICE OF THE DISCIPLE: "Let me take it upon myself to speak to the Lord, I who am but dust and ashes" (Genesis 18:27). If I think of myself more highly than I ought, my sins bear witness against me and your holy light reveals my darkness.... You illuminate my true self—what I am, what I have been and where I am going. I am nothing, but I did not realize it. Left to my own devices, I bring everything to nothing; my own strength is actually weakness. When my own weight sinks me to the depths, you lift me up and graciously embrace me. That is the wonder of free grace.[1]

Your love does all this for me. You reach out to me before I even sense your presence;[2] you support me and uphold me in all my needs. When I focused all my attention on myself, I lost myself.[3] When I sought to love you above all things, I found both myself and you. And by loving you as I ought, I reduced myself to true humility. For you, most blessed Lord, deal with me graciously and above all I deserve, above all I even dare to hope or ask.

Blessed are you, O my God, for although I am unworthy of any benefits, you shower me with your grace and you are at work for good in my life all day long. Grace even surrounds the ungrateful and those who are far from you.[4]

Turn us all to you, O Lord, that we may be thankful, humble, and holy; for you are our power, and our strength, and our salvation.[5]

1 *The Westminster Catechism*, a short manual of instruction for Christians written by English and Scottish church leaders in the 1640s, maintains that the chief purpose of human beings is to glorify God and enjoy God forever. This is the primary way in which we serve God.

2 Many Christian writers use water imagery to describe God's love. This fountain is a source of living water, springing up eternally.

3 The child of God who has experienced God's steadfast love, mercy, and care yearns to serve God with his or her whole heart. Forgiven people become forgiving people; beloved children of God become lovers of humanity.

CHAPTER 7

☐ God's Service

THE VOICE OF THE DISCIPLE: O Lord, I am not ashamed to shout and will not be silent. I will exult in my God, my Lord, and my King, exclaiming: "O how abundant is your goodness that you have laid up for those who fear you ... !" (Psalm 31:19). How wonderful you are to those who love you. How glorious you are to those who serve you with their whole heart. Truly, they contemplate your beauty and joy overflows in their hearts. You bestow your lavish gifts on those who love you. I can testify boldly to the wonder of your love, for when I did not yet exist, you made me, when I strayed far from you, you brought me back again, that I might serve you (Genesis 1:27).[1]

O Fountain of everlasting love, what shall I say about you?[2] How can I ever forget the One who has never forsaken me? You have shown mercy to me—your servant—beyond all my expectations. You befriended me and cared for me far more than I ever deserved.... "What shall I return to the Lord for all his bounty to me?" (Psalm 116:12). I want to serve you all the days of my life![3] If I could just give you one full day of worthy service! Truly, you are worthy of all service, of all honor and everlasting praise. Truly, you are my Lord, and I your humble servant; I am determined to serve you with all my might. I will never grow weary of praising you. I have but one wish: whatever I lack, O Lord, supply it that I may serve you better.

1 Jesus's disciples asked him to teach them how to pray. They recognized their need to apprentice themselves to a master who knew how to pray well. Jesus's pattern of prayer acknowledges that God always has our best at heart. Note the many times Christ refers to the will. The thrust of this prayer echoes his own poignant words in the Garden of Gethsemane, "[Y]our will be done" (Matthew 26:42).

2 Thomas articulates a dynamic conception of grace. Grace can be found within. God is present and at work in the human heart. Grace works to redeem and to heal. The disciple's prayer implies that it can be lost. Cooperating with God's grace, however, pleases God and leads to communion.

3 Howard Thurman wrote extensively on holiness of heart and prayed that the last vestige of his own will would no longer be in conflict with the Spirit of God.

4 The writer of John's Gospel loved the image of abiding in Christ. In John 15 he records Jesus's own image concerning the church—the vine and the branches—which emphasizes intimacy and productivity. Abiding or resting in God implies deep peace, joy, and an overwhelming sense of well-being, gifts then offered to others for the sake of Jesus.

CHAPTER 8

☐ Human Desires

THE VOICE OF CHRIST: My beloved, when you pray, say: Lord, you know what is best. Give whatever you will, how much you will, and when you will. Deal with me as you think best—whatever pleases you and brings you honor. Place me wherever you wish and let your will be done in me. I am in your hand. Chart the direction of my life as you desire. Behold, I am your servant, prepared for all things, for I do not want to live only for myself.[1]

THE VOICE OF THE DISCIPLE: Grant me your grace, O most merciful Jesus, that it may be with me, and work within me, and remain with me to the end.[2] Grant me always to desire and will that which is most acceptable and pleasing in your sight. Let your will be mine, and let my will conform perfectly to yours.[3] Let my deepest desires all be one with yours, and let me only desire what you will for me in my life.

Grant that I may die to all things in this world and embrace humility and meekness for your sake. Above all, grant that I may rest in you. Quiet my heart as I abide in you, for you are my true peace and my only rest.... In this peace, found only in the one, true God, may I sleep and rest forever.[4] Amen.

1 The sentiments of the previous chapter spill over into Thomas's reflections on trust.

2 It would be difficult, indeed, to turn control of one's life over to someone who did not care about you. But the prophet Jeremiah affirms God's benevolent intentions for the faithful: "For surely I know the plans I have for you, says the Lord, plans for your welfare and not for harm, to give you a future with hope" (29:11).

3 What a profound litany of praise!

4 While the ability to entrust one's life to Christ at the outset of the journey is important, the companionship of Christ along the way also confirms and shapes the disposition of trust in the heart.

5 The English Puritan tradition, with its emphasis on covenant, embraced this spirit. Drinking deeply from this spiritual well, John and Charles Wesley prayed, "I am no longer my own, but thine. Put me to what thou wilt, rank me with whom thou wilt. Put me to doing, put me to suffering. Let me be employed for thee or laid aside for thee, exalted for thee or brought low for thee. Let me be full, let me be empty. Let me have all things, let me have nothing" (the historic Covenant Prayer).

CHAPTER 9

☐ Entrusting All to God

THE VOICE OF CHRIST: My beloved, permit me to order your life as I see fit, for I know what is best for you.[1]

THE VOICE OF THE DISCIPLE: Lord, what you say is true. Your concern for me is greater than all the care I can provide for myself (Matthew 6:30). I am willing to turn everything over to you because I am certain to fall if I stand on my own. So do with me whatever you please, Lord, and align my will perfectly with your own. I know that all of your purposes for me are good.[2] Make my way difficult; your name be praised. Make my path easy; your name be praised. Offer comfort to me; your name be praised. Afflict me; your name be praised.[3]

THE VOICE OF CHRIST: My beloved, this must be your disposition if you want to walk with me.[4] You must be as ready to suffer as to rejoice, to be poor and needy as full and rich.

THE VOICE OF THE DISCIPLE: Lord, I willingly suffer whatever you send my way. I am willing to receive good and evil, sweetness and bitterness, joy and sorrow from your hand, and give you thanks for it all.[5] Keep me from all sin, and I will fear neither death nor hell. I know that, as long as I stay close to you, you will not send me away, blot me out of the book of life, or harm me through any trial.

1 In the extended prayer of the disciple that follows, Thomas strikes the keynote of his heart religion—abiding rest in God.

2 Even religious people take great delight in many of these aspects of life. While none of these are bad in and of themselves, they can become sources of pride. To place one's security in any of these things is a dangerous illusion.

3 Thomas catalogs the eternal and reliable qualities of the Divine.

4 This statement echoes the famous dictum of St. Augustine, drawn from the opening paragraph of his *Confessions* (I.1.1).

CHAPTER 10

☐ Resting in God

THE VOICE OF THE DISCIPLE: Rest in the Lord above all things and in all things, O my soul, for the Lord is the everlasting rest of the saints.[1]

Grant me, O most gracious and loving Jesus, to rest in you above all things: above all health and beauty, above all glory and honor, above all power and dignity, above all knowledge and cleverness, above all riches and arts, above all joy and gladness, above all hope and promise, above all merit and desire, above all gifts and favors that you can pour out upon us, above all joy and triumph that our minds can receive and feel,[2] and finally, above all the angels and archangels, and above all the hosts of heaven, above all visible and invisible things.

For you, Lord God, are above all things the best: you alone are most high, most powerful, most full and sufficient; you alone are most sweet and overflowing with comfort, most lovely and loving, most noble and glorious, in whom all things work together for good (Romans 8:28), and most perfectly, and ever have been and shall be....[3] Surely my heart cannot truly rest, unless it rests in you.[4]

(continued on page 97)

5 The mystic longs for complete union with God, even absorption into God. Love makes the soul take flight and soar into the embrace of the God of love. The soul yearns for this kind of communion.

6 Ponder this poignant paradox.

7 The disciple begs Christ to come. This prayer echoes the very last word of the Christian scriptures—*maranatha*—"Come, Lord Jesus" (Revelation 22:20).

8 "Wisdom of the Father" is a title given to Jesus. Wisdom is different from knowledge. Wisdom has to do with what we do with knowledge—how we use it. Jesus helps us understand the significance of things. He is the key to meaning and purpose.

O my beloved Jesus, the most pure lover, the supreme ruler over all things: "O that I had wings like a dove! I would fly away and be at rest!" (Psalm 55:6). O when shall it be granted me in quietness of mind to see how sweet you are, my Lord and my God! When shall you and I be united so fully in love that I no longer feel myself, but you alone, above all sense or measure, in a manner not known to any other?[5]

O Jesus, the brightness of eternal glory, the comfort of the vanquished soul, in whom my tongue is silent, and yet in silence speaks.[6] Come without delay, O Lord. Come to your humble servant and fill me with gladness. Stretch forth your hand and deliver me from all my troubles. Come, O come! for without you I have nothing in which to rejoice; for you are my joy, and without you, my table is empty.[7]

Your works are all good, your judgments ever true, and your governance of all things guided compassionately by your kind providence. Praise, therefore, and glory, be to you, O Wisdom of the Father![8] Let my mouth, my soul, and all creatures together, praise and bless your holy name.

1 This string of scriptural quotations identifies selflessness, humility, and obedience as the character traits that lead to inner peace. These virtues define our freedom as the children of God. Paradoxically, we experience true freedom when we abandon self to the higher causes of God's will and way. The historic Collect for Peace in the Anglican tradition describes service to God as the Christian's perfect freedom.

2 The mystical path to union with God entails purification, illumination, and ultimate communion—peace in God and self.

3 No one is strong enough to make this ascent without help. The pilgrim particularly needs assistance to overcome those barriers and pitfalls that stand in the way of progress towards love.

4 Thomas employs the images of creation and re-creation by grace in this eloquent prayer.

CHAPTER 11

☐ Causes of Peace

THE VOICE OF CHRIST: My beloved, now I will teach you the way of peace and true liberty. Endeavor to bend your will to the will of others (John 6:8). "Do not seek your own advantage, but that of the other" (1 Corinthians 10:24). "Sit down at the lowest place" (Luke 14:10). Pray continually, "Your kingdom come. Your will be done, on earth as it is in heaven" (Matthew 6:10). Behold, the person with this disposition will find true peace and freedom in life.[1]

THE VOICE OF THE DISCIPLE: Enlighten me, O blessed Jesus, with a clear, shining, inward light, and drive out all the darkness in my heart.[2] Properly direct my wandering thoughts and drive away those temptations that continue to assault me. Fight strongly for me and conquer these evil forces and enticing lusts, that peace may reign in my heart and praise ascend to your holy court from my lips.[3] Command the winds and the storms in my life to cease. Say to the sea, "Peace! Be still!" (Mark 4:39), and to the north wind, "Stop blowing," and there will come a great calm.

"O send out your light and your truth" (Psalm 43:3) that they may shine on the earth; for I am as the earth, like "a formless void" (Genesis 1:2), unless you enlighten me. Pour out your grace from above. Let your heavenly dew materialize in my heart. Supply streams of devotion to water the face of the earth, that it may bring forth good and excellent fruit....[4] Join me to yourself with an inseparable bond of love, for only you can satisfy the longing heart.

1 This advice sounds extremely harsh. But Jesus offered this same guidance to a man who asked what he must do to inherit eternal life. He said to him, "If you wish to be perfect, go, sell your possessions, and give the money to the poor, and you will have treasure in heaven; then come, follow me" (Matthew 19:21). St. Antony (251–356 CE), the founder of Christian monasticism, took these words literally, gave away all his possessions, and began a life of apostolic poverty.

2 A life fixated on self leads to despair, hopelessness, and death. God created us to share life and love with others. Self-absorption, however, impedes or even destroys healthy relationships.

3 Ironically, the things we possess can end up possessing us. The more things you have, the more control things have over your life. St. Francis of Assisi resolved to own nothing so that nothing could own him.

4 In radical consumerist cultures, many fall prey to this seductive trap.

5 All four of these action verbs are important in relation to God. If we seek God, we will find God; if we find God, we will enjoy God; if we enjoy God, we will love God.

CHAPTER 12

☐ Dangers in Self-Absorption

THE VOICE OF CHRIST: My beloved, give away all you have to others and retain nothing for yourself.[1] Self-absorption does more harm to you than anything else in the world.[2] In proportion to the love and affection you have for things, they will cling to you more or less. If your love is pure, however, no material things can ever hold you in bondage.[3] Do not covet what you cannot have. Do not permit your attachment to material possessions to steal your inner sense of freedom.

If you seek this or that, or if you yearn to be here or there for the sake of your own pleasure or to acquire more and more, you will never rest or be free from care. There will always be something else, something better, that you want.[4] Likewise, there will always be someone in every situation to tempt you to covet more.

THE VOICE OF THE DISCIPLE: Strengthen me, O God, by the grace of your Holy Spirit (Psalm 51:12). Give me the power to be strengthened inwardly (Ephesians 3:16) and empty my heart of all inordinate desire and anxiety, so that I will not be drawn away by things simply to satisfy myself.... Lord, give me heavenly wisdom to seek, find, enjoy, and love you above all things.[5]

1 The understanding described here is far more than intellectual knowledge. Those who know God's love have experienced it, felt it, and celebrated its transforming power. If you know this God, you need nothing else.

2 We should love all things only as means to loving God more fully.

3 The disciple addresses God as "Radiance Divine." This prayer celebrates light. Strong verbs reveal the penetrating nature of God's light, which pierces, cleanses, cheers, illuminates, invigorates, and fills. One of Charles Wesley's great hymns, *Christ Whose Glory Fills the Skies*, picks up these themes: "Visit then this soul of mine, pierce the gloom of sin and grief, fill me Radiancy Divine, scatter all my unbelief; more and more thyself display, shining to the perfect day."

CHAPTER 13

☐ God's All-Sufficiency

THE VOICE OF THE DISCIPLE: My God and my all, you are everything to me, the source of all my happiness. O sweet and blessed Word! ... My God and my all! One need say no more to those who understand.¹ For those who love you, how pleasant it is to repeat your praise. When you are near, all things are blessed; when you are absent, nothing is right. You quiet the heart and offer peace and joy to all. You enable us to appreciate all you have made. You inspire our praise of all creation. But we love nothing properly unless we cherish it for your sake.² For anything to be blessed, your grace must be present. It must be seasoned with the sweetness of your wisdom.

O Radiance Divine, surpassing all created light, pierce the innermost part of my heart with the beams of your brightness from above. Cleanse, cheer, illuminate, and invigorate my spirit with all its powers that I may cling to you with ecstatic joy and triumph. O when will that blessed hour come, when I shall be filled with your presence, and you will be all in all to me!³

1 Note the emphatic vision of total commitment to God in these statements—"whole heart ... whole trust ... whole heart."

2 True freedom comes to those who seek to grow in their faith or trust in God and cultivate Christ-like dispositions in their lives.

3 Christian discipleship entails more than a one-time commitment. Jesus says, "Take up [your] cross daily and follow me" (Luke 9:23). Those who seek to follow Jesus not only entrust their lives to his care, but also walk in the way of Jesus. Eugene Peterson (b. 1932), translator of the acclaimed Message Bible, published a classic devotional volume entitled *A Long Obedience in the Same Direction*, which underlines this theme.

4 Jesus, the Second Person of the Trinity, emptied himself of everything but love when he entered human history as Jesus of Nazareth (Philippians 2:5–11). This self-emptying made him totally transparent to God. He calls us to empty ourselves in the same way—to become naked—so as to let God's love shine through us without distortion or impediment.

CHAPTER 14

☐ Freedom of Heart

THE VOICE OF CHRIST: My beloved, renounce yourself and you will find me. Relinquish your self-will, your possessions, and resign yourself to my will without presumption or pride.... Surrender your sense of entitlement, in both great and small things, and constantly seek to strip control from self. Otherwise you can never abide in me and I in you (John 15:4). Your own will stands as a barrier to our abiding fellowship. Some resign themselves, but do not give their whole heart to me. They do not put their whole trust in God and, therefore, they assert their autonomy all the more. Some offer their whole heart to me at first, but succumb to the assault of various temptations and return to their illusions of self-determination.[1] They find it impossible, therefore, to grow in grace or to cultivate virtue.[2] These seek freedom and purity of heart in vain. Genuine liberation comes only from an entire resignation of self and a daily sacrifice of self to me and my way.[3]

I have often told you, and now I tell you again, "Relinquish your own will and surrender yourself to me and you will find peace of heart. Give all for all. Seek nothing for yourself. Require nothing in return from others. Abide in me, without hesitation, and you will be mine and I will be yours. Your heart will be free and darkness will have no power over you. Let this be your prayer—let this be your desire—that being stripped of all selfishness, you may follow the naked Jesus in your own nakedness,[4] and that dying to yourself, you may live eternally with me."

1 Thomas returns to the theme of human brokenness and our desperate need for God.

2 Early church fathers, like the famed bishop of Lyons, St. Irenaeus (d. 202), distinguished between the image and the likeness of God. Both God's image and likeness must be restored in fallen humanity. To be like God means to be good, just, and holy—to let love govern all our thoughts, words, and actions.

3 Certainly, Thomas bases his diagnosis of the human condition on the scriptural witness, but he has also learned from his own experience and his observation of others.

4 Despite his pessimistic view of fallen humanity, Thomas does not despair because God transforms and heals all who turn to Jesus. Over against his pessimism with regard to the condition of human beings, he embraced a profound optimism in the power and sufficiency of God's grace.

CHAPTER 15

☐ Brokenness in Life

THE VOICE OF THE DISCIPLE: "What are human beings that you are mindful of them, or mortals that you care for them?" (Psalm 8:4). What has anyone done to deserve your grace? Lord, do I really have any cause to complain or lash out at you when I do not get what I want? Surely, Lord, I am nothing. I can do nothing.[1] I am not capable of any good on my own. I am broken and inclined to unhealthy, self-destructive choices. Unless you help and inwardly instruct me, I become altogether cold and distant from you.

"But you, O Lord, are enthroned forever; your name endures to all generations" (Psalm 102:12). You put your love in action through goodness, justice, and holiness.[2] You speak and act with great wisdom. I, on the other hand, am more ready to go backward than forward, always fickle and divided in all my ways.[3] But whenever you offer me your helping hand I feel transformed. Only you can help me, without the aid of any other, and strengthen my heart and mind so as to rest in you alone, resolute, unchanging, and secure.[4]

O my truth, my mercy, my God, most blessed Trinity; to you alone be praise, honor, power, and glory for evermore.

1 All knowledge finds its source in the One who is wisdom, power, and grace. Those who participate in the genuine knowledge of God experience unity and peace.

2 Prophesying seven centuries before the coming of Christ, Zephaniah warned against the coming doom that would overtake Judah because of the corrupt and violent rule of King Manasseh. He called on the children of God to return to Yahweh and to live in a way that would be pleasing to God. In the same way that God's judgment falls on the sinful nation in the time of Zephaniah, so too, God will judge the hearts of all people one day. Thomas alludes, therefore, to the manner in which God searches and judges the human heart, using the metaphor of the lamp from Zephaniah that illuminates sin and wickedness.

3 Christ admonishes the disciple to treasure love and intimacy with God above everything else.

4 Christ describes himself as an internal source of wisdom. The indwelling Christ offers truth, forgiveness, spiritual discernment, and goodness.

CHAPTER 16

☐ Wisdom

THE VOICE OF CHRIST: My beloved, do not be persuaded by fine speeches and subtle arguments, "for the kingdom of God depends not on talk but on power" (1 Corinthians 4:20). Guard against sin, for that fight will be of greater value to you than your ability to navigate difficult intellectual arguments. When you have studied and mastered many things, return to this one, basic principle: "I am the one who teaches knowledge to humankind" (Psalm 94:10) and gives greater understanding to babes than can be taught by any human.[1]

The time will come when the Master of masters will appear, Christ, the Lord of the heavens, to examine the conscience of everyone. At that time, the Lord "will search Jerusalem with lamps" (Zephaniah 1:12) and expose the hidden things in the darkness, and the tongues of those who think they are wise will be silenced.[2]

I teach without the noise of words, without the clash of differing opinions. I teach others to despise worldly possessions and hold the current age in disdain, to seek the everlasting and embrace things eternal, to shun honors and suffer injuries, to place all hope in incarnate love and to desire nothing but divine intimacy.[3] Above all, I invite others to love ardently. I dwell within every human heart; the teacher of truth, the searcher of the soul, the discerner of thoughts, the promoter of good works,[4] distributing "gifts that differ according to the grace given to" each person (Romans 12:6).

1 Thomas encourages those who have advanced along the way of Jesus. Such a glimpse into eternity comes to those who have enjoyed the company of Christ as a routine encounter—moment by moment—learning and embracing his ways.

2 This is a profound description of how God interacts with God's children: God visits, stirs, and sustains. This is a Trinitarian vision. In Jesus God comes into human history. Through the Spirit God stirs our hearts. The One who created all things sustains everything through love.

3 God offers the gift of a vision to encourage those who seek to persevere to the ultimate goal.

CHAPTER 17

☐ Eternal Life

THE VOICE OF CHRIST: My beloved, whenever God gives you a vision of eternal life, open your heart wide and receive this holy inspiration with your whole soul.[1] Offer ardent thanks to God for dealing with you so kindly, for visiting you so mercifully, for stirring you so fervently, and for sustaining you so powerfully.[2] This gift of God lifts you up when your own weight would topple you to the ground and drown you in the things of the earth. You can never obtain such a vision on the basis of your own thought or effort; rather, it is a gift of heavenly grace and divine favor. Such a vision helps you to progress in holiness and humility and prepares you for future battles of the spirit.[3]

1 A genuine experience of God's love pulls us out of enslavement to ourselves and focuses our attention on others.

2 The disciple struggles throughout life in the paradoxical tension of the presence and hiddenness of God. It is not always clear why God seems so near at times and so distant under other circumstances. Regardless, anyone who has trusted God's loving presence yearns for it always. Nothing sustains the soul more than the experience of God's presence, in part because human beings long for connection with God and one another.

3 We shrink from the mystery of God's omniscience and the challenge of human suffering. Everyone has struggled with the questions, "Why do bad things happen to good people?" "What is the source and purpose of suffering?" Thomas offers no simple answer; rather, he surrenders everything to God in every circumstance. He lives in hope despite the harsh reality of human suffering.

CHAPTER 18

☐ Surrender

THE VOICE OF THE DISCIPLE: Lord God, Holy Father, be blessed, both now and for evermore. Whatever you will is done and whatever you do is good. I rejoice in you, not in myself, nor in any other thing, for you alone are the source of my gladness. You are my hope and my crown, my joy and my honor, O Lord.

I long for the joy of your peace. I earnestly crave peace for your children, that they may be led by you in the light of your consolation.[1] If you give peace, if you pour your holy joy into my heart, then my servant-soul overflows with gladness and sings your praise forever. But if you withdraw yourself from me ... I will bow my knees and beat my breast, and I will long for those days when your radiance shone on my face and you protected me under the shadow of your wings (Psalm 63:7).[2]

O righteous God, ever to be praised, my time of trial has come. Behold, adored Father, I consider it an honor to suffer something for your sake. Merciful God, extolled throughout the ages: in the midst of this present persecution—which you foreknew from all eternity should come—I surrender all and live inwardly for you forever.[3] I have become little, despised, humble, weak and worn down in the sight of my adversaries, that I might rise again with the morning of the new light and be glorified in heaven. Holy Father, you have appointed it and will have it so. Let all things be fulfilled at your command.

1 This profound sense of sin overwhelms the reader. Those who have a proper self-understanding are deeply conscious of and openly acknowledge their broken state. Spiritual healing and recovery begin with this important first step.

2 The poetic fifty-fifth chapter of Isaiah brings the vision of the prophet to a triumphant climax. Isaiah celebrates God's mercy and forgiveness. The wonders of divine grace seem like impossibilities to many people, and God's gracious offer of salvation to everyone appears to be beyond the comprehension of any person. But God's range of vision is universal and includes all people. God's understanding of the human heart surpasses our own knowledge of ourselves. Isaiah's message to every age is that God will always have mercy and forgive because this is God's nature.

3 John Wesley defined repentance as true self-understanding. The Greek word for repentance, *metanoia*, can also be translated "conversion." The idea is that, facing one direction, some force turns you around so that you face and move in the opposite direction.

4 This theme pervades the Psalms. Scholars describe a number of these sacred poems, including the Psalm quoted here, as "Penitential Psalms" (typically 6, 32, 38, 51, 102, 130, and 143). The concern for repentance and confession of sin dominates these songs.

CHAPTER 19

☐ True Self-Knowledge

THE VOICE OF THE DISCIPLE: Lord, I am not worthy of your comfort or your presence. You are just to abandon me to my guilt and shame. Even if I were able to shed a sea of tears, I could never make amends for what I have done. I deserve nothing but your just punishment, because I have grievously offended you and have sinned greatly in many things.[1] But you, O merciful God, "not wanting any to perish" (2 Peter 3:9), show the depth of your goodness and fulfill your promises, for your ways are not like our ways (Isaiah 55:8).[2]

What shall I say, guilty as I am, and full of all confusion? I have nothing to say but this, "I have sinned, Lord. I have sinned. Have mercy on me and pardon me. Permit me just enough time to express my grief before I go into the land of darkness, a land covered with the shadow of death." Is it not true that all you require of guilty and contrite sinners is that they humble themselves before you? Hope of forgiveness arises from genuine repentance and humility of heart.[3] The troubled conscience is reconciled to God. The favor of God, which was lost, is recovered. God and the penitent sinner "greet one another with a holy kiss" (Romans 16:16).

"The sacrifice acceptable to God is a broken spirit; a broken and contrite heart, O God, you will not despise" (Psalm 51:17).[4]

✣ Theologians have debated the relationship between nature and grace since the dawn of humanity. What is the condition of the human being? Is the human being by nature good or evil? Thomas draws a sharp contrast between human nature and divine grace. In other words, he believes that, while fallen human nature pulls us down, God's grace lifts us up. We need—and God offers—grace for us to experience restoration, spiritual health, and wholeness. His vision of the human condition, as expressed here and elsewhere in this work, sounds very much like St. Augustine. A corrupted human will, focused on its own self-interest, has no hope of correcting itself. Only God's grace can redeem fallen human nature in his view.

CHAPTER 20

☐ Nature and Grace

THE VOICE OF CHRIST: My beloved, pay close attention to the difference between fallen human nature and divine grace.... The fallen nature is crafty. It seduces, embroils, and deceives, always working for its own end. But grace walks in simplicity, authenticity, and purity, always acting purely for God's sake.

Nature fears shame and contempt, but grace rejoices to suffer reproach for the name of Jesus. Nature loves ease and rest, but grace cannot be idle and willingly embraces hard work. Nature seeks to have those things that are ostentatious and beautiful and abhors that which is common or coarse. But grace delights in plain and humble things and accepts the ordinary.

Nature is covetous and revels in receiving more than giving, but grace is bountiful and generous to all, shuns private interests, is content with enough, and thinks that it is more blessed to give than to receive. Nature inclines to the creature, to the ways of the flesh, and to foolishness and wandering, but grace identifies with the Creator and goodness, renounces the ways of the world, controls the desires of the flesh, guards against going astray, and blushes at notoriety. Nature seeks outward comfort and the delight of the senses, but grace seeks comfort in God alone, and delights in the highest good above all visible things.

☩ In the previous chapter Thomas articulates a very pessimistic view of fallen human nature. He immediately reminds the reader here, however, that we are created in God's image and likeness. Whereas Thomas expresses pessimism with regard to fallen human beings, he is profoundly optimistic about the power of God's grace to redeem, heal, and restore. Divine grace heals the human sickness.

1 St. Paul draws a sharp contrast between the law of sin and death and the law of righteousness, particularly in chapters 7 and 8 in his letter to the church at Rome. If sin reigns in a person's life, the consequence is spiritual death. But those who seek intimacy with God, desire purity of heart, and unite themselves with Jesus will experience abundant life. The opening verse of Romans 8 brings one of St. Paul's arguments in this regard to a climax: "There is therefore now no condemnation for those who are in Christ Jesus. For the law of the Spirit of life in Christ Jesus has set you free from the law of sin and of death" (8:1–2).

2 Note the variety of positive images, including feminine images, that Thomas uses for grace: handmaid, teacher, radiance, solace, expeller, nurse, and mother.

3 Persons restored by God's grace reflect their newfound faith and spiritual health by doing good.

☐ The Optimism of Grace

THE VOICE OF THE DISCIPLE: O Lord, my God, who has created me after your own image and likeness (Genesis 1:26): grant me that grace which is necessary for salvation, that I may overcome my diseased nature. I feel in my flesh the law of sin contradicting God's law of righteousness and love....[1] O Lord, without your grace I can do nothing. "I can do all things through him who strengthens me" (Philippians 4:13). O heavenly grace, indeed, without which our most worthy actions are nothing. Arts, riches, beauty, strength, wit, eloquence, are of no value with you, O Lord, apart from your grace.

Your grace is the handmaid of truth, the teacher of discipline, the radiance of the heart, the solace of affliction and sorrow, the expeller of fear, the nurse of devotion, and the mother of tears.[2] What am I without grace, but a withered branch and an unprofitable stock, only meant to be cast away. Let your grace, therefore, O Lord, always envelope me, and follow me, and make me ever diligent in good works, through Jesus Christ your Son. Amen.[3]

1 In this paragraph, Thomas provides an amazing exposition of Jesus's famous "I am" saying recorded in John 14:6. This statement may have given rise to the earliest description of Jesus's disciples as followers of ' the Way." Union with Jesus is the way to God. Jesus declares himself to be the ultimate reality—the Truth. One of the dominant themes of John's Gospel is the Life all find in Jesus.

2 Note the inversion of the trilogy of way, truth, and life in this statement. Here is Thomas's simple prescription for the spiritual life.

3 Thomas roots apprenticeship to Jesus in the cross. The cross functions as his primary paradigm for the faithful life. His cross-centered Christology emphasizes the lengths to which God's love will go to redeem and restore beloved, but erring, children.

4 The faithful disciple of Jesus takes on the shape of the cross—lives a cruciform life. The vertical beam reaches up continually to God, but is firmly rooted in this world. The horizontal beam reaches out to others with a loving embrace.

CHAPTER 22

☐ Self-Denial

THE VOICE OF CHRIST: "Follow me" (Matthew 16:24). "I am the way, and the truth, and the life" (John 14:6). Without the way, there is no clear path; without the truth, there is no knowledge; without life, there is no living. I am the way, which you ought to follow; the truth, which you ought to trust; the life, for which you ought to hope. I am the way inviolable, the truth infallible, the life eternal. I am the straight way, the supreme truth, the authentic life—the blessed life, the uncreated life. If you remain in my way, you will know the truth, and the truth will set you free, and you will receive everlasting life.[1]

"If you wish to enter into life, keep the commandments" (Matthew 19:17). If you want to know the truth, believe me. If you desire to be my disciple, renounce yourself (Luke 9:23).[2] "Those who love their life lose it, and those who hate their life in this world will keep it for eternal life" (John 12:25). "Whoever does not carry the cross and follow me cannot be my disciple" (Luke 14:27).[3] Only the servants of the cross share the bliss and the light of God's love.

THE VOICE OF THE DISCIPLE: Lord Jesus, as you have said and promised, so let it be unto me. I have received the cross, I have received it from your hand. I will bear it, and bear it until death, as you have laid it upon me. Truly, the life of a Christian is shaped by the way of the cross.[4] It is the only true guide to paradise. I have begun. May I never go back.

1 Jesus—the One who has suffered on behalf of others—fully recognizes the painful realities of life. He realizes the importance of encouragement to those who suffer, and he offers it freely. Suffering and death are not the end for the believer; rather, resurrection and life always triumph in the rule of God.

2 The disciple acknowledges how the presence of Jesus means everything in times of suffering. In our own experiences of suffering, often the simple presence of an empathetic friend brings comfort and solace that supersedes words. In the presence of an empathetic friend, we feel safe. Thomas employs this beautiful metaphor—the safe harbor—to express the ultimate peace and calm of the life lived to God. He articulates a vision of salvation that we could describe as "homecoming."

3 Thomas looks to the joys of heaven and prays for a happy voyage into God's eternal embrace. But that embrace actually begins in this life. We need not wait for a life that follows this experience.

CHAPTER 23

☐ Encouragement

THE VOICE OF CHRIST: My beloved, patience and humility in adversity are more pleasing to me than much comfort and devotion in prosperity.... All is not lost if you feel yourself often afflicted or grievously tempted. I am the One who will comfort and strengthen those who mourn. I will raise up unto divine glory those who have felt the sting of suffering and pain.[1]

THE VOICE OF THE DISCIPLE: Lord, blessed be your word; it is "sweeter also than honey, and drippings of the honeycomb" (Psalm 19:10). If you were not by my side to comfort me with your holy words in the midst of my trouble and grief, what would I do? What matters most is how I find my way into your safe harbor through the troubled seas of this life.[2] Grant me a good end. Grant me a happy passage out of this world and into the next! Be mindful of me, O my God, and direct me in the right way to your eternal realm. Amen.[3]

✝ Much of life is shrouded in mystery. Questions plague us from cradle to grave concerning the reason why things are the way they are. Perhaps the most difficult questions in life revolve around the human experience of suffering and evil—the issue of theodicy. Great theologians and philosophers have sought to tackle these kinds of questions, offering alternative answers to these perplexing quandaries in life. Thomas cautions against too much speculation in these matters. He seems to prefer residing in the mystery rather than finding rational explanations for questions he considers beyond our reach.

1 What person has not asked questions like these about life?

2 No one will ever receive complete answers to these questions. These are mysteries in life that are inscrutable, but nonetheless perplexing.

3 Thomas looks to the Psalms in order to find a fitting response to these questions—a simple affirmation of God's righteousness and truth.

4 This is not to say that the questions are invalid or should not be asked. But struggling with life's big questions without an abiding trust in God only leads to frustration and failure.

CHAPTER 24

☐ Deep Mysteries

THE VOICE OF CHRIST: My beloved, beware of efforts to understand the deep mysteries of this life and the secret judgments of God. Why is this one left behind and that one shown such great favor? Why is this one so greatly afflicted and that one so effortlessly advanced?[1] These questions are beyond your reach. No intellectual exercises or debates can search out fully the judgments of God.[2] When the enemy, therefore, suggests these kinds of questions to you, or some curious people place them before you, simply answer with the prophet: "You are righteous, O Lord, and your judgments are right" (Psalm 119:137). And again, "The ordinances of the Lord are true and righteous altogether" (Psalm 19:9).[3] God's judgments are to be acknowledged, not debated.[4] Many of these mysteries cannot be comprehended through the use of our limited reason.

1 These are simple but profound definitions of heaven and hell. Note how they are defined in terms of the presence or absence of God. Heaven is intimacy with God; hell is separation from God.

2 In the experience of the disciple, God is the only reliable source of these critical qualities that give life meaning and purpose. Despite our struggle to remain faithful to Christ, he always remains faithful to us!

3 Christ provides the model of always putting others first.

4 Jesus relates to and sustains his disciples through his actions. Note these positive and powerful action verbs: assist, help, strengthen, comfort, instruct, keep. Ponder what any one of these might mean on an average day, at work, with your children, among those who annoy you, when deadlines crush your joy.

5 Those who seek to imitate Christ pledge their faith to God and implore God's mercy so that they might be instruments of God's grace to others. Book III concludes with a universal prayer of supplication, asking God to comfort the heart and to guide the soul safely to its everlasting home.

CHAPTER 25
☐ Hope and Trust in God Alone

THE VOICE OF THE DISCIPLE: Where you are, there is heaven; death and hell are wherever you are not.[1] You are my deepest desire. Therefore, I cannot but sigh, and cry, and pray, to you. For I have no one in whom I can put my trust. You are the only one who can help me, my God. You are my hope. You are my trust. You are my comfort. You are faithful to me in all things.[2]

Everyone else seeks their own salvation; you only seek mine and translate all things to my good....[3] I put my whole trust in you, therefore, O Lord God, my only hope and refuge.... My closest friends cannot assist, nor strong helpers aid, nor wise counselors give proper guidance, nor the books of the well-educated comfort, nor any wealth deliver, nor any secret or pleasant place defend, if you are not there to assist, help, strengthen, comfort, instruct, and keep me.[4]

You are the goal of all that is good, the height of life, the depth of wisdom. My greatest strength is to trust in you above all things. "To you I lift up my eyes" (Psalm 123:1). In you, O my God, the Father of all mercies, I put my trust. Bless and sanctify my soul with your heavenly blessing, that it may be made your holy dwelling place and the seat of your eternal glory. May nothing ever be found in this holy temple that may offend your eyes.... Protect and keep the soul of your servant in the midst of so many dangers, and by your grace accompanying me, direct it in the way of peace to the country of everlasting light. Amen.[5]

BOOK IV
The Sacrament of Holy Communion

✝ God offers grace to all in the fullest possible expression of divine love through a sacred meal. This act of love in Christian worship—known in different traditions as the Lord's Supper, Holy Communion, Eucharist, or the Mass—involves eating bread and drinking wine together. While a multi-faceted symbolic meal, three aspects of this liturgical act stand out. The Lord's Supper is a memorial of the suffering and death of Jesus. This dimension of the Sacrament focuses on remembrance. Indeed, Jesus said, "Do this in remembrance of me" (Luke 22:19). The meal connects the faithful with the love of God in the Crucified One who sets us free. The Eucharist is a meal of thanksgiving. The meal is a sign and means of grace that celebrates the real presence of the risen Lord Jesus. Christian disciples experience his presence anew by faith as they gather around the table. Holy Communion is a foretaste of a great heavenly banquet in which all the faithful will one day share in glory. The meal is a pledge of a future filled with hope.

1 Each of these texts from the Christian scriptures relates to the Sacrament in one way or another. Jesus provides spiritual food that nourishes, sustains, and unites the community of faith. He gives himself freely.

2 The disciple acknowledges the truth of these words because they come from Truth itself. The words of Christ encourage. These are promises the disciple takes to heart.

3 Jesus's command comes in the form of an invitation. He invites all to the Gospel feast—a banquet characterized by lavish hospitality. Note the powerful inversion of the text from Matthew's Gospel, "Come to me, all you ... all of you, come to me."

CHAPTER 1

☐ Reverence for Christ

THE VOICE OF CHRIST: "Come to me, all you that are weary and are car-rying heavy burdens, and I will give you rest" (Matthew 11:28). The bread that I will give for the life of the world is my flesh (John 6:51). "Take, eat, (Matthew 26:26), this is my body that is for you. Do this in remembrance of me" (1 Corinthians 11:24). "Those who eat my flesh and drink my blood abide in me, and I in them" (John 6:56). "The words that I have spoken to you are spirit and life" (John 6:63).[1]

THE VOICE OF THE DISCIPLE: These are your words, O Christ, the everlast-ing Truth. Because they are your words and true, I receive them all in faith with thanksgiving. They are yours and you have spoken them; they are mine also because you have spoken them for my salvation. I willingly receive them from your mouth, that they may be all the more deeply imprinted on my heart. Your words encourage me because they are filled with grace, filled with sweetness and love.[2]

You command me to come to you with confidence. I want to share my life with you here and in eternity, so you invite me to receive the food of immortality. "Come to me, all you that are weary and are carrying heavy burdens," you say to me, "and I will give you rest" (Matthew 11:28). O sweet and friendly words in the ear of sinners. That you, my Lord God, invite the poor and needy to participate in your most holy body! But who am I that I should presume to approach you, O Lord? Behold, the heaven of heavens cannot contain you, and yet you say, "All of you, come to me."[3]

(continued on page 133)

4 Note the emphasis on the heart once again. While beyond our intellectual grasp, Jesus's gift stirs up the emotions and fans the heart-flame of love.

5 God's grace may not be visible, but trust enables the disciple to experience grace as love.

6 Thomas refers to the Sacrament as a "means of grace." Such means are outward signs, words, or actions ordained by God as channels whereby God conveys life-giving grace to God's beloved children. It is around the table of the Lord that God offers grace to all in the fullest possible expression of love divine.

7 Participation in Christ leads to holiness of heart and life. In the Sacrament, the community of faith realizes righteousness in a double sense. It both recognizes the righteousness of Christ and experiences genuine holiness by uniting believers to the Righteous One.

8 Thomas laments the loss for those who have eyes but cannot see, who have ears but cannot hear.

9 A final enunciation of the central theme of this chapter.

O God, the invisible Creator of the world, you are so unbelievably good to us! How sweetly and graciously you offer good gifts to your beloved children, to whom you give your own self to be received in this Sacrament! This exceeds all understanding! This strongly draws the hearts of the devout and inflames their affections.[4]

Those who are faithful to Jesus receive your hidden grace and love in this Sacrament.[5] But the unbelieving and those who are slaves to sin miss this great blessing! You offer us your grace and strength in this Sacrament. Through this means of grace you restore what we lost through sin;[6] you restore our native beauty disfigured by sin. Your sacramental grace is sometimes so powerful, that both our minds and our weak bodies feel an increase of strength as we receive you into our lives.

Jesus is our sanctification and redemption.[7] He comforts us in our pilgrimage through life. He brings the saints safely home. How unfortunate that so few seriously consider this holy mystery, which fills the heavens with joy and preserves the whole world. How hard the hearts and blind the eyes of those who do not contemplate seriously so unspeakable a gift![8]

Thanks be to you, gracious Jesus, the everlasting Shepherd, who refreshes us poor exiles with your precious body and blood and invites us to receive these mysteries with the words of your own mouth: "Come to me, all you that are weary and are carrying heavy burdens, and I will give you rest."[9]

1 Jesus offers himself in the Sacrament to those in need. It is the Lord's table.

2 Note the contrast between these titles for Jesus and the needs of weak human beings. Jesus provides living water for thirsty servants; the King welcomes his creatures with open arms. The God of all comfort meets and consoles those who mourn as they come to the meal.

3 This threefold description characterizes the God of goodness, mercy, and love who claims the hearts of the faithful.

4 This portrait of God stands in stark contrast to that in the minds of many people—a God who is authoritarian, critical, and distant. This God of hospitality, anticipation, and generosity eagerly awaits the response of beloved children.

CHAPTER 2

☐ God's Goodness and Love

THE VOICE OF THE DISCIPLE: Confident of your goodness and great mercy, O Lord, I come to you, sick, hungry, and thirsty.[1] I come to the fountain of life, to the King of heaven, a needy servant to my Lord, a creature to my Creator. I come in mourning to you, my blessed Redeemer, in need of your mercy and comfort.[2] ... I confess my unworthiness; I acknowledge your goodness. I praise your mercy and give thanks to you for your transcendent love. You come to me for your own sake, not for any merit of mine, that your goodness may be better known to me, your love more abundantly shown, and your gracious condescension the more eminently displayed.[3]

Behold, you offer me hospitality, even though I am not worthy so much as to look upon you. Behold, you come with eager anticipation to me and invite me to your banquet. You give me the food of heaven and bread of angels to eat, which is nothing other than your very self—"the bread of God is that which comes down from heaven and gives life to the world" (John 6:33).[4]

(continued on page 137)

5 | Christians have many different views concerning the presence of Jesus in the Sacrament. In 1215, the Fourth Lateran Council approved the doctrine of transubstantiation, declaring that the essence of the bread and wine are transformed into the essence of Jesus's body and blood in this meal. There can be little doubt that Thomas subscribed to this understanding of the "real presence" of Jesus. On the opposite end of the spectrum, some of the more radical Protestant traditions believe in what could be called a "spiritual presence" of the risen Lord. Mediating positions affirm both a physical and spiritual presence, but without the conception of a transformation of the elements. The Lutheran view maintains that Jesus is "in, with, and under the elements." John Calvin (1509–1564), the Genevan reformer, argued a "true presence" of Jesus in which believers experience the power of Jesus through the instrumentality of the Spirit. The Wesleys posited a relational presence that unites the believer, body, soul, and spirit, with Jesus. Across this wide spectrum of belief, the main point and Thomas's conviction, is that we meet God in this holy meal.

6 | St. Paul reminds the Corinthian Christians that "as often as you eat this bread and drink the cup, you proclaim the Lord's death until he comes" (1 Corinthians 11:26). The Sacrament reminds the community of faith about the central place of Jesus's death on the cross.

7 | At the table, the faithful remember the event of the crucifixion in such a way that it becomes real in the present moment. Rather than a passive memorial of what Jesus has done for sinful people on the cross in the past, by means of the Sacrament, the faithful enter into the mystery of that sacrificial death, receive a present forgiveness of their sins, and participate in the transforming love of the risen Jesus.

How amazing, my Lord God, that you come to us in the elements of bread and wine![5] You are the Lord of all things and have no need of anything or anyone, yet you are pleased to dwell in us through your Sacrament. Preserve my heart and body undefiled, that I may often celebrate your mysteries with a cheerful and pure conscience. May I receive this gift—which you have ordained and instituted for your honor—as a perpetual memorial.[6]

The love of Christ is never diminished and the greatness of his sacrifice is never exhausted. Earnestly contemplate, therefore, the mystery of your salvation. It ought to seem to you as great, new, and joyful as if the same day Christ first descended into the womb of the virgin, was made a human being, or, hanging on the cross, did suffer and die for the salvation of all humankind.[7]

1 The story of Zacchaeus in Luke's Gospel (19:1–10) underscores Jesus's desire to eat with outcasts. He often chooses the least likely as his table companions. In this case, he welcomes the hospitality of a hated tax collector.

2 Participation in the Sacrament unites the believer with Jesus by faith.

3 In the same way that our bodies need physical food, our souls need spiritual nourishment. Jesus supplies the spiritual food we need in the Sacrament.

4 Thomas portrays Jesus as one who longs to fill the faithful with good gifts. Since Jesus is our greatest friend and extends an invitation to join him at the banquet, who would not want to meet him there at every opportunity?

5 In 1 Corinthians 11:28, St. Paul stresses the need to approach the Eucharistic meal with an inclusive vision of the community of faith—the body of Christ. He is not so much concerned about one's ability to understand the theology of the Sacrament as he is concerned about the ability to live with others in love and to view all as equals around the table of the Lord.

CHAPTER 3

☐ Frequent Communion

THE VOICE OF THE DISCIPLE: Behold, O Lord, I come to you that I may be comforted by your gift and overjoyed at your holy banquet. "In your goodness, O God, you provide for the needy" (Psalm 68:10). You are all I can or ought to desire; you are my salvation, my redemption, my hope, my strength, my honor, and my glory! "Gladden the soul of your servant, for to you, O Lord, I lift up my soul!" (Psalm 86:4). I desire to receive now, O Lord, with devotion and reverence. I long to welcome you into my house that, with Zacchaeus, I may be blessed by you and numbered among the children of Abraham (Luke 9:1–8).[1] My soul hungers and thirsts to receive your body and blood; my heart desires to be united with you.[2]

Give me yourself and it suffices, for there is no comfort in any but you. I cannot live without you and your constant presence. Therefore, I must come to you often and receive you for the welfare of my soul. If I were deprived of your heavenly food I would collapse along the journey.[3] For this very reason, the most merciful Jesus, while preaching to the people and curing their diseases, said to the disciples, "I do not want to send them away hungry, for they might faint on the way" (Matthew 15:32). Deal with me in the same way now, divine Provider, for you have promised to feed and comfort the faithful in your blessed Sacrament.[4] You are the beautiful reflection of the soul, and whoever participates in the meal in a worthy manner[5] will eat with you in everlasting glory.

(continued on page 141)

139

6   The word "Eucharist" means "thanksgiving." The meal fills all who participate with inexpressible joy, overwhelming happiness, and ecstatic praise. The believer looks forward to communion with Jesus as a spouse yearns for intimacy with his or her beloved.

7   In the face of God's unfathomable love, words cannot express the depth of feeling in the vanquished heart—the heart overcome with the joy of communion with Christ.

You promise to come to a humble soul and satisfy her hunger with the fullness of your divine presence! Happy the mind and blessed the soul that receives you with devout affection, O Lord God, and is filled thereby with spiritual joy! How awesome the Lord entertained by the soul! How beloved a guest! How pleasant a companion! How faithful a friend! How lovely and glorious a spouse![6] The soul embraces the One who is to be loved above all that is beloved and above all things that may be desired. Let all mortal flesh, and all the heavenly hosts, keep silence before you, O Lord.[7] All the praise and beauty that we are able to offer comes from your bounty. It cannot equal the beauty of your name, the glory of which we cannot comprehend.

1 Distraction—inattentiveness or indifference—during prayer or sacred moments plagues many sincere spiritual pilgrims. Thomas demonstrates how one does not solve this problem by bending oneself into submission by sheer force of the will; rather, simple honesty and transparency before a loving God help focus one's spirit on the sacred.

2 This is an interesting image. God waits to bless those who gather at the table, and the blessings that await everyone are hidden, like the pearl of great price in Jesus's parable of the kingdom in Matthew 13:41–51.

3 Some Christians describe the Sacrament as a "holy mystery," or simply "the Mystery." More happens in the meal than meets the eye. God works supernaturally to connect with people in a multitude of ways.

4 Note the gravitation here to the language of the mystic—deeply longing, melting, and overflowing.

5 A large catalog of amazing benefits accompanies participation in the Sacrament.

CHAPTER 4
☐ A Table of Blessing

THE VOICE OF THE DISCIPLE: My Lord God, reach out to your servant with the blessings of your steadfast love, that I may approach your glorious Sacrament with all reverence and awe. Lift up my heart to you and deliver me from a distracted mind.[1] Visit me with your salvation that I may taste the sweetness of your grace, which lies hidden in this Sacrament as in a fountain.[2]

Enlighten my eyes to behold so great a mystery, and strengthen me to believe it with steady faith.[3] You are at work here and not any human power; this meal is your sacred institution, not a human invention. No one can comprehend these things, which surpass the understanding even of angels. What, therefore, shall I, unworthy sinner, dust and ashes, be able to comprehend of so high and sacred a mystery!

O Lord, at your command I come to you with simplicity of heart, with hope and reverence, and truly believe that you are present in this Sacrament. You want me to receive you and to be united with you in love. I beg your mercy, therefore, and crave your special grace, that I may wholly melt and overflow with love to you and never seek comfort anywhere else.[4] This most blessed and grace-filled Sacrament is the health of my soul and body, the remedy of all spiritual weakness. Through this holy mystery my vices are cured, my passions bridled, temptations overcome, grace is infused, virtue begun and increased, faith confirmed, hope strengthened, and love inflamed.[5]

(continued on page 145)

6 Note the typical threefold pattern in the structure here—three powerful descriptions of Jesus related to three perennial concerns of the child of God. This God yearns to comfort, encourage, and protect all the faithful.

7 In this concluding paragraph, Thomas exploits mystical imagery related to water and fire, and connects them intimately with the personal needs of all human beings. His language is poetic. His expectation is great.

You bestow many benefits in the Sacrament upon your beloved ones, upon those who receive in faith. O Protector of my soul, Repairer of human frailty, and Giver of inward peace, you impart to your children comfort in distress, hope in despair, and protection in disturbance.[6] You inwardly refresh and enlighten them with new grace. Those who have come to the table heavy and distressed depart refreshed with the bread of heaven and the cup of blessing; they find themselves transformed.... You are a fountain always full and overflowing, a fire ever burning and never decaying.

Your blessings are so great that I cannot draw out of the full fountain itself, nor drink my fill.[7] But I will set my lips to the chalice of your grace that I may draw out at least some small drop to quench my thirst and not be wholly dried up. Although I am far from holy and not so inflamed with love as the angels above, I will endeavor after some small spark of divine fire by participating with humility in this life-giving Sacrament. Whatever I lack, O merciful Jesus, most holy Savior, bountifully and graciously supply. For you have promised to visit all who respond to your call: "Come to me, all you that are weary and are carrying heavy burdens, and I will give you rest" (Matthew 11:28).

1 Thomas somewhat inexplicably begins to use this title for Christ and will continue to do so through the remainder of Book IV.

2 The point is simple—no one participates in any way in the Sacrament because he or she is worthy. All are invited, not because of who they are or what they have done, but because of who God is. All come in response to grace.

3 The priest or pastor blesses the bread and wine of this sacred meal. God invests the common and ordinary with divine significance.

4 The church has always been careful to maintain that it is God who works in the Sacrament and not human beings. The Sacrament is valid, not on the basis of the one who celebrates, but on the basis of the work of God accomplished through the power of the Spirit.

5 This refers to the act of ordination.

6 Those who embrace a vocation to celebrate the Sacrament shoulder an awesome responsibility. The calling to feed God's people necessarily entails a quest for personal holiness as well.

CHAPTER 5

☐ The Dignity of the Sacrament

THE VOICE OF THE BELOVED:[1] If you had the purity of an angel or the holiness of John the Baptist, you would still not be worthy to receive or celebrate this Sacrament.[2] No one has earned the right to consecrate the Sacrament of Christ or to receive the bread of angels for their food. Those who preside over the Sacrament—an honor not even given to angels—exercise an office filled with mystery. For priests alone, duly ordained of God and set apart by the church, have power to consecrate the body of Christ.[3] The minister of God uses God's word by God's command and appointment, but God authors the event and works invisibly.[4]

Consider seriously the awesome responsibility of those set apart by the imposition of the hands of the bishop.[5] You are made a priest and consecrated to celebrate. Be faithful and devout, therefore, as you offer this sacrifice to God; exercise your ministry in a way that is above reproach. Virtue ought to characterize the life of the minister who provides an example of right living in holiness for others. Your conversation should never be common or ordinary, but like that of the angels in heaven.[6]

The priest represents Christ on earth. Prostrate yourself before God, then, and pray humbly for yourself and the whole people of God. Pray without ceasing till you obtain grace and mercy. When you celebrate the Sacrament, honor God, rejoice with the angels, edify the church, help the disciples of Jesus, and partake of God's goodness.

1 Priests must strive for purity. The proper exercise of this office entails serious introspection and a desire to please God in all things.

2 Oblation is another word for sacrifice. Those who seek to be the faithful children of God must offer the entirety of their lives to God. But until sacrifice is seen as opportunity, we misunderstand the rich radiance of God and miss out on freedom found with God.

3 Thomas returns here to a central theme in Book I, namely, purity of intention.

CHAPTER 6

☐ Examination of Conscience

THE VOICE OF THE BELOVED: Above all things, the minister of God ought to come to celebrate and receive this Sacrament with great humility of heart, lowly reverence, and a pious intention to honor God. Examine your conscience diligently, therefore, confessing the secrets of your heart so that God might cleanse you fully, leaving no barrier between you and the altar.[1]

Offer your whole self upon the altar of your heart as a living sacrifice, holy and acceptable to God, to the honor of God's name. Such an oblation will enable you to celebrate and receive the Sacrament in a worthy manner, for the only sacrifice necessary in Holy Communion is the offering of one's whole heart to God.[2] God offers pardon and grace to all who seek it with purity of intention.[3] "I have no pleasure in the death of the wicked, but that the wicked turn from their ways and live" (Ezekiel 33:11). "For I will be merciful toward their iniquities, and I will remember their sins no more" (Hebrews 8:12).

1 The writer of the Epistle to the Hebrews claims that Jesus "entered once for all into the Holy Place, not with the blood of goats and calves, but with his own blood, thus obtaining eternal redemption" (9:12). One of the ancient prayers of the church observes how Jesus stretched out his arms on the hard wood of the cross that the entire world might come within the reach of his saving embrace. God calls the disciples of Jesus to assume this posture in life as well.

2 God desires the yielded hearts of Jesus's followers more than anything else.

3 In these two preceding sentences, Thomas uses the word "wholly" four times. Christ gives himself without reserve to us and thereby models our own wholehearted commitment to God.

CHAPTER 7

☐ Sacrifice and the Meal

THE VOICE OF THE BELOVED: As I willingly offered up myself to God my Father for your sins, my hands being stretched forth on the cross and my body naked, so that nothing remained in me that was not wholly turned into a sacrifice, so too you ought also to offer up yourself willingly to me every day, as a pure and holy oblation, with all your power and affection, in as full a manner as you can.[1] The only thing I require of you is that you commit your whole self to me. Nothing else that you sacrifice really matters to me at all; I do not seek your gift, only yourself.[2]

In the same way that it would not suffice if you had everything but me, so neither can it please me to have all your gifts if you do not offer yourself. Offer up yourself to me, therefore, and give yourself wholly to God, and I will accept your offering. Behold, I offered up myself wholly to my Father for you, that I might be wholly yours and you wholly mine.[3] But if you abide only in yourself and do not offer yourself up freely to my will, your sacrifice is not complete, neither will the union between us be perfect. A free offering up of yourself into the hands of God, therefore, ought to take priority over everything else, if you truly desire to obtain freedom and grace. Very few enjoy genuine freedom and spiritual illumination, because they cannot deny themselves without reserve. My saying is unalterable: "None of you can become my disciple if you do not give up all your possessions" (Luke 14:33). If you desire to be my disciple, therefore, offer up yourself wholeheartedly to me.

1 In prayer, the disciples of Jesus offer themselves fully to God. They commit themselves wholeheartedly to the Lord of all.

2 Wholehearted surrender to God involves the confession of all one's sins. We offer our brokenness to God. But such a surrender includes the acknowledgment of our goodness as well. We offer our good works to God. The good in life offered freely to God entails every aspect of the disciple's life of prayer—adoration, repentance, thanksgiving, and intercession—the deepest moaning of the heart. We offer our very souls to God.

3 He alludes here to the ultimate prayer—*kyrie eleison*—Lord, have mercy (from the Liturgy of the Mass).

CHAPTER 8

☐ Offering All to God

THE VOICE OF THE DISCIPLE: "The earth is the Lord's and all that is in it, the world, and those who live in it" (Psalm 24:1) I desire to give myself to you as a free offering and to remain yours forever. O Lord, in the simplicity of my heart, I offer myself to you today—a sacrifice of perpetual praise, to be your servant forever.[1]

I offer you all my sins and offences, O Lord, on the altar of your mercy.... Consume them all with the fire of your love and wash out all the stains of my sins. Cleanse my conscience from all offences and restore your grace to me, which I lost by sin. Forgive all my offences and receive me mercifully with the kiss of peace!

I also offer you all that is good in me,[2] although there is very little and it is far from perfect. Amend and sanctify it. Accept all my good works and perfect them more and more.

I offer you all my prayers, especially for those who have wronged, grieved, or slandered me in any way and made my life uncomfortable or unbearable. I pray also for all those whom I have at any time troubled, grieved, or scandalized by words or deeds, wittingly or unawares. Please forgive all our sins and offences against one another. Take from our hearts, O Lord, all jealousy, indignation, wrath, and contention, and whatever may preclude or diminish love. Have mercy, O Lord, have mercy on those who crave your mercy.[3] Give grace to them who stand in need and grant that we may be counted worthy to enjoy your grace and attain life everlasting. Amen.

1 The Eucharist is not an end in itself. It is a means to a greater end, namely, the fullest possible communion with God.

2 The Sacrament prefigures the glory of the heavenly banquet to come. As St. Paul observes, "Now we see in a mirror, dimly, but then we will see face to face. Now I know only in part; then I will know fully" (1 Corinthians 13:12). "The ray shall rise into a sun," Charles Wesley sings, "the drop shall swell into a sea."

3 Participation in the Word and Sacrament—light and food—defines the Christian life. As it is in the physical world, so it is in the spiritual realm. Through this potent conjunction God reaches out to us and we come to know God through the bread of life.

CHAPTER 9

☐ An Essential Meal

THE VOICE OF THE DISCIPLE: In this world I ought to be content with the light by which I live and to walk by faith until the day of everlasting brightness breaks forth and all shadows pass away. But when that which is perfect comes, the sacraments shall cease.[1] For the saints in heavenly glory need no place of divine-human encounter; rather, they rejoice without ceasing in the presence of God. Beholding God's glory face to face (Genesis 32:30), and "being transformed into the same image from one degree of glory to another" (2 Corinthians 3:18), into the image of the incomprehensible deity, they taste the Word of God made flesh as he was from the very beginning and will be forever.[2]

I require two things in this life without which everything would be insufferable. While I remain in this body, the two things essential to my life are food and light. Therefore, you have given your sacred body and blood to this weak creature to nourish soul and body (John 6:51) and you have set your Word "as a lamp to my feet and a light to my path" (Psalm 119:105). Without these two things, I could not live well. The Word of God is the light of my soul and your Sacrament is the bread of life (John 6:48).[3]

(continued on page 157)

4 This is one of the most memorable images in *The Imitation of Christ*. God feeds us from two tables.

5 Thomas breaks into a prayer of thanksgiving, celebrating the teachings of the church—the community's reflection on the Word of God— and the banquet, in which the faithful encounter God's eternal love.

6 Jesus offers his life on the cross as a sacrifice. The Lord's Supper commemorates this great act of self-giving love.

7 In the practice of most Christian communities, those who participate in the Sacrament lift their cupped hands to receive the bread and take the cup in hand to drink the wine.

These may also be called the two tables, set on one side and on the other, in the storehouse of the holy church. One is the holy altar that holds the holy bread—the precious body of Christ. The other is the holy table of your Word, the divine law that contains the teachings of the true faith and leads to the holy of holies behind the veil.[4]

Thanks be to you, O Lord Jesus, Light everlasting, for the table of holy doctrine, which you have given to your servants through the prophets, apostles, and teachers of the faith. Thanks be to you, Creator and Redeemer of all things, who prepares a great banquet to manifest your love to the whole world (Luke 14:16).[5] You set the table, not with the typical lamb of sacrifice, but with the most sacred body and blood of your Son (John 6:53–56).[6] All the faithful rejoice in this holy meal, for it replenishes them to the fullest with the cup of salvation (Psalm 23:5), pours heaven into their hearts in this passing world, and fills all within the family of God with the paradise of love.

The eyes that behold the body of Christ ought to sparkle with the radiance of simplicity and chastity. The faithful lift pure hands to receive the Creator of heaven and earth.[7] As the ancient law prescribed: "You shall be holy, for I the Lord your God am holy" (Leviticus 19:2).

1 This statement affirms the grace-filled character of this meal. Jesus offers himself not to those who are worthy, good, and perfect, but to the unworthy—the least, last, and lost.

2 The main theme of this great parable of the banquet is joy—the sheer joy of being invited. The theme of humility runs through the parable as well. God issues the invitation because of our need. We come to the table because we are hungry. All people hunger—all of us some of the time, and some of us all of the time. Those who have little testify to the indignity and pervasiveness of hunger. The rich starve inwardly, while appearing fat and satisfied on the outside. Nevertheless, God extends the invitation to all.

3 The participants' simple desire to come is much more important to God than the way they have prepared themselves to receive Jesus.

4 This purpose or goal—to cultivate unity, grace, and love—dominates Thomas's view of the Sacrament.

CHAPTER 10

☐ Preparation for Communion

THE VOICE OF THE BELOVED: I invite you to my table, not because of who you are or what you have done, but because of my good grace and pleasure.**1** When you are invited to a lavish banquet, go and sit down at the lowest place (Luke 14:10) and give thanks for your blessings. Likewise, if you are hosting a feast, invite the poor and "you will be blessed, because they cannot repay you" (Luke 14:6).**2** Do whatever you are able to do diligently; receive your beloved Lord God, not out of custom or a sense of obligation, but with awe, reverence, and affection. I am the One who has called you. I have commanded the feast and will supply whatever is lacking in you. Simply come and receive me.**3**

If God blesses you with a great reverence for the Sacrament, give thanks; God gives the gift not because you are worthy, but because God lavishes mercy on you. On the other hand, if your spirit is dry and cold toward God, continue to pray—ask, seek, and knock (Luke 11:9)—persist in prayer until you are ready to receive some crumb or drop of saving grace. You need me; I do not need you. Do not come to the table to satisfy me, for I come to expand your vision of holiness and cultivate your character. Come, therefore, and permit me to shape you more fully into my own image and likeness. The Sacrament provides an opportunity for you to be united with me, to be filled with grace, and to be inflamed with love for the amendment of your life.**4**

(continued on page 161)

159

5 | The disciple strikes the keynote of intimacy with God, using the metaphors of lover and friend to describe the nature of our relationship with God.

6 | This mystical language describes the deepest yearnings of the disciple of Jesus and provides a segue into Thomas's discussion of union with Christ.

THE VOICE OF THE DISCIPLE: I look forward to intimate fellowship with you at the table, O Lord, in the same way that the lover yearns to speak with her beloved and a friend anticipates a great party with his friend.[5] I pray that I may be wholly united with you and shun all earthly diversions that seduce my heart and soul. I want to commune with you often and learn increasingly how to desire heavenly and eternal things. Ah! Lord God! When shall I be wholly united to you and swallowed up in you completely?[6]

✠ More than anything else, the mystic yearns for union or communion with God. Whereas the medieval mystics describe the path that leads to mystical union in great detail in their writings, St. Teresa of Avila was one of the first to attempt a systematic analysis of this spiritual process. In this devotional classic, she described the journey of soul through seven stages, or rooms in a castle, ending with union with God. Practical mystics like Thomas conceive the Sacrament as an essential practice integral to this pilgrimage into the heart of God. This pivotal chapter provides an opportunity to explore and delight in this goal.

1 A series of statements, beginning with the words, "in truth," describe Jesus as the source of all love, peace, and joy.

2 Note these ecstatic exclamations related to the character of God revealed in Jesus.

3 Nothing supersedes the heart because the heart symbolizes the whole self.

CHAPTER 11

☐ Union with Christ

THE VOICE OF THE DISCIPLE: You in me and I in you (John 15:4); grant us both to continue as one.

In truth,[1] you are my beloved, "distinguished among ten thousand" (Song of Solomon 5:10), in whom my soul is blessed to dwell all my days. In truth, you are my Prince of Peace, whose peace surpasses all understanding (Philippians 4:7) and whose rest transcends work, and sorrow, and misery in life. In truth, you are the Bread of Life who demonstrates your devotion to your children and promises to feed them with the bread that comes down from heaven, filled with sweetness and joy.

O unspeakable grace! O inestimable mercy! O infinite love, singularly bestowed to the children of God! "What shall I return to the Lord for all his bounty to me" (Psalm 116:12), for such an unfathomable expression of love?[2] What can I give him, poor as I am? I have nothing to offer that can ever suffice. Yet what I can I give him, give my heart![3] And that I give wholly to you, O God, and without reservation. My whole being would rejoice with exceedingly great joy if I were perfectly united to God. Then God will say to me, "If you truly desire to be with me, I will be with you." And I will answer, "Promise, O Lord, to remain with me, and I will gladly be with you. This is my whole desire, that my heart may be united to you forever."

✝ In the following two chapters Thomas deals realistically with human feelings. He deals with the underlying questions, "What if I do not feel anything when I participate in the Sacrament? What if I have no sense of God's presence when I receive Communion?" These are real questions that he seeks to answer by focusing, not on transitory human feelings that shift and change so easily, but on God's steadfast promise and presence.

1 Thomas does not fear blatant honesty with God about one's spiritual state.

2 In such times of dryness and coldness, the beloved simply begs for the mercy of God.

3 In the Sacrament, God consistently offers and manifests the three theological virtues (1 Corinthians 13:13). Participation in the Eucharist shapes these virtues—faith, hope, and love—as well as the cardinal virtues of prudence, justice, temperance, and courage—in the faithful disciple.

CHAPTER 12

☐ Communion

THE VOICE OF THE DISCIPLE: "O how abundant is your goodness that you have laid up for those," O Lord, "who fear you" (Psalm 31:19)! When I remember some devout persons who come to your Sacrament with the greatest devotion and affection, O Lord, I am confounded and blush within myself, that I come with such heaviness and coldness of heart to your table.[1] I lament the fact that I remain so dry and devoid of any love, that I feel no sense of passion or overwhelming desire as many devout persons, who earnestly long after you, the living Fountain, with their whole heart and soul. Be merciful to me, blessed Jesus, holy and gracious Lord, and grant me, your poor, needy creature, to feel in this holy communion, sometimes at least, something of your tender love and mercy.[2] As a consequence of tasting your heavenly manna, strengthen my faith, increase my hope in your goodness, and inflame my love to the extent that it can never decay.[3]

1 Everything in this meal is about grace. But the beloved must reciprocate God's wholehearted offer with wholehearted desire. In this masterful statement, Thomas describes the dynamic, relational nature of God's grace and the way in which we appropriate it in our lives.

2 The pastoral side of Thomas emerges here as he offers practical, spiritual guidance.

3 As we approach the conclusion of this devotional classic, Thomas returns to the theme of heart religion and the centrality of wholehearted commitment to Jesus.

4 The verbs in these statements define the practical mysticism of the author. The Christian life consists of seeing, being filled (particularly with wonder), having one's heart enlarged—about experiencing God forever.

CHAPTER 13
□ Humility and Sacramental Devotion

THE VOICE OF THE BELOVED: You ought to seek the grace to participate in the Sacrament with Christ wholeheartedly, to ask for it earnestly, to expect it patiently and confidently, to receive it gratefully, to keep it humbly, to work with it diligently, and leave to God the nature and manner of your communion with Christ when it comes.[1] Most importantly, humble yourself before God when you feel little or no inward devotion; be neither too dejected nor grieved inordinately by your coldness. God often gives in a moment what you have awaited for a long time.[2] God sometimes bestows, in the end, what was deferred in the early stages of your life of prayer. Sometimes a little thing hinders and hides grace.... But if you remove this, be it great or small, you shall have all you desire.

As soon as you commit yourself to God with your whole heart, and seek not this nor that for your own pleasure or will, but fix yourself wholly on God, you will find yourself united and at peace.[3] ... Then you shall see, and be filled, and wonder, and your heart will be enlarged within you, because you will sense that the hand of the Lord is with you. If you seek God with your whole heart you will enjoy this overwhelming peace. You will experience an unspeakable union with God when you receive the holy Eucharist.[4]

1 This prayerful confession mirrors a prayer in the ancient Sarum Rite, the liturgy for Holy Communion used in Salisbury and southern England from the eleventh century. Thomas Cranmer (1489–1556), famous archbishop of Canterbury and Christian reformer, translated this Collect for Purity and included it in his first edition of the *Book of Common Prayer* in 1549:

> Almighty God, to whom all hearts be open, all desires known, and from whom no secrets are hid; Cleanse the thoughts of our hearts by the inspiration of thy Holy Spirit, that we may perfectly love thee, and worthily magnify thy holy Name; through Christ our Lord. Amen.

2 Thomas paints a memorable portrait of the child of God who longs for God's grace. The punctuated images that follow illustrate deep desire and call for serious reflection.

3 The "Prayer of Great Thanksgiving," the central element of the Eucharist in common Communion liturgies today, includes a dialogue known as the *Sursum Corda* in which the priest and people proclaim: "Lift up your hearts. We lift them up to the Lord. Let us give thanks to God. It is right to give our thanks and praise."

CHAPTER 14

☐ Yearning for God's Grace

THE VOICE OF THE DISCIPLE: O most holy and loving Lord, whom I desire to receive with all heart, you know my weaknesses and the circumstances of my life, how I am oppressed, grieved, tempted, troubled, and defiled. I come to you for help. I yearn for your comfort and relief. Almighty God, my heart is fully open to you. You know my deepest desires. I can hide nothing from you.[1] Only you can perfectly comfort and help me. You know what I need most to be whole and happy. Only you can cultivate virtue in my life.

Behold, I stand before you, poor and naked, asking for your grace and imploring your mercy.[2] Refresh your hungry beggar. Warm my heart with the fire of your love. Enlighten my blindness with the radiance of your presence. Turn all earthly things to bitterness for me, all things grievous into patience, all created things into contempt and oblivion. Lift my heart to you in heaven,[3] and turn my wandering heart away from the things of this earth. From now on, fill me with the sweetness of your presence, for you alone are my meat and my drink, my love and my joy, my glory and my good.

(continued on page 171)

4 The ultimate prayer of every faithful Christian.

5 This melting refers primarily to God's action upon the human heart. God must melt the heart of stone in order to prepare it to become the dwelling place of love.

6 Thomas conceives God as a glowing, burning, flaming, and enlightening fire of love.

O that your presence would wholly inflame, consume, and transform me into your Christ-like child.[4] Make me one spirit with you by the grace of inward union (1 Corinthians 6:17) and by the melting influence of steadfast love.[5] Never let me leave your table hungry or thirsty, but mercifully accept my sacrifice and fill me, just as you have nourished your saints through the ages. How wonderful it would be if I were able to die to myself fully and live only for you, inflamed with your love. The fire of your love burns eternally, nothing can ever put it out. Purify my heart and enlighten my understanding with your glowing presence.[6]

✠ In this concluding chapter, Thomas provides a summative review of the primary themes and concerns related, not only to his sacramental vision, but to his whole conception of the Christian life. His description of heart, religion, humility, purity of intention, gratitude, commitment, servanthood, and steadfast love inspires others to embrace their true identity as the children of God.

1 Throughout *The Imitation of Christ*, Thomas uses Mary, the Mother of Jesus, as a model of obedience and self-giving love. The Annunciation (Luke 1:26–38) and the Magnificat (Luke 1:46–55), in particular, reveal her character and capture the spirit Thomas seeks to inculcate in the believer.

CHAPTER 15

☐ Fervent Love

THE VOICE OF THE DISCIPLE: With great devotion and steadfast love, with the affection and fervor of my whole heart, I desire to receive you, O Lord, as many saints and devout persons have desired you when they received your Sacrament. They were most pleasing to you in holiness of life and unparalleled in devotion. O my God, my everlasting love, my whole good, my never ending happiness, I would gladly receive you with the most vehement desire and most worthy reverence that any of the saints ever had or could feel.

Although I am unworthy to have all those feelings of devotion, yet I offer my whole heart to you as if I alone had all those inflamed desires. Whatever a holy mind can conceive and desire, all this, with the greatest reverence and most inward affection, I offer and present to you. I reserve nothing to myself, but freely and most willingly sacrifice myself and all that I am to you. My Lord God, my Creator and my Redeemer, I desire to receive you this day with such affection, reverence, praise, and honor; with such gratitude, worthiness, and love; with such faith, hope, and purity, as the blessed Mother of Jesus received and desired you when she humbly and devoutly answered the angel who declared to her the mystery of your incarnation: "Here am I, the servant of the Lord; let it be with me according to your word" (Luke 1:38).[1]

(continued on page 175)

2 In the Eucharistic liturgy common to many Christian traditions today, faithful disciples join their voices with the whole company of heaven and faithful people throughout time in a hymn of praise to God: "Holy, Holy, Holy Lord, God of power and might. Heaven and earth are full of your glory. Hosanna in the highest. Blessed is he who comes in the name of the Lord. Hosanna in the highest."

3 Thomas asks for the community of faith to pray for him, identifying himself with the prodigal son in one of Jesus's most memorable stories of mercy, grace, and love (Luke 15:11–32).

4 During the crucifixion of Jesus, one of the criminals put to death with him pleaded, "Jesus, remember me when you come into your kingdom" (Luke 23:42). Thomas identifies with this request. He asks Jesus to remember his humble soul—the soul of one who sought to imitate Christ in all things.

I want to be inflamed with such great and holy desires and to offer myself up to you with my whole heart. So I offer also and present to you the joys, affections, ecstasies, the supernatural illuminations and heavenly visions of all devout hearts, with all the virtues and praises celebrated by all creatures in heaven and earth, that through all of this you may be worthily praised and glorified forever.

Receive, my Lord God, my wishes and desires to give you infinite praise and abundant blessing, which are justly due to you because of the multitude of your unspeakable gifts to me. I yield all to you and desire to sacrifice every day and moment to your glory. I invite all the angels and archangels, all the company of heaven, and all your devout servants here on earth to give thanks and praise together with me.[2]

Let the "great multitude that no one could count, from every nation, from all tribes and peoples and languages" (Revelation 7:9) praise you and magnify your holy name with the highest joy and most fervent devotion. Let all that reverently celebrate the Holy Sacrament find grace and mercy at your hands and pray humbly for me, your prodigal child.[3] And when they shall have obtained the fullness of your grace and joyful union with you, and depart from your sacred, heavenly table fully comforted and most marvelously refreshed, let them remember my humble soul.[4]

Notes □

Introduction

1. See www.practicingourfaith.org/what-are-christian-practices.

2. Bernard of Clairvaux, *On Loving God*, X.28, in Robert Walton, trans., *Treatises II* (Kalamazoo, Michigan: Cistercian Publications, 1980), 120.

3. John Wesley, *A Plain Account of Christian Perfection* (London: William Pine, 1766).

4. George Stanhope, *The Christian's Pattern: Or, A Treatise of the Imitation of Christ, in Four Books* (London: Printed for M. Gillyflower et al, 1698).

Suggestions for Further Study ☐

Billy, Dennis J., ed. *The Imitation of Christ: A Spiritual Commentary and Reader's Guide.* Notre Dame: Ave Maria Press, 2005. A helpful commentary on the translation of the text by William Creasy.

Chilcote, Paul Wesley, ann. *John & Charles Wesley: Selections from Their Writings and Hymns—Annotated & Explained.* Woodstock, VT: SkyLight Paths Publishing, 2011. A recent anthology of selected writings of the Methodist founders, with probing facing-page commentary that provides instruction about the spiritual life.

Constable, Giles. *Three Studies in Medieval Religious and Social Thought.* Cambridge: Cambridge University Press, 1995. An examination, in part, of the growing interest in the humanity of Jesus in the late medieval period.

Hyma, Albert. *The Christian Renaissance: A History of the Devotio Moderna.* 2nd ed. Grand Rapids: Archon Books, 1965. One of the most influential earlier works in America on this topic.

Kelley, Joseph T., ann. *Saint Augustine of Hippo: Selections from* Confessions *and Other Essential Writings—Annotated & Explained.* Woodstock, VT: SkyLight Paths Publishing, 2010. With fresh translations and probing facing-page commentary, illustrates how Augustine's keen intellect, rhetorical skill, and passionate faith reshaped the theological language and dogmatic debates of early Christianity.

Leclercq, Jean. *The Love of Learning and the Desire for God: A Study of Monastic Culture.* Translated by Catharine Misrahi. New York: Fordham University Press, 1982. A classic study of the monastic tradition that provides a contextual backdrop to the ethos of the Brothers and Sisters of the Common Life.

Post, R. R. *The Modern Devotion: Confrontation with Reformation and Humanism.* Leiden: Brill Academic Pub., 1968. The definitive study of the *devotio moderna* in its historical context.

Tinsley, Ernest John. *Imitation of God in Christ: An Essay on the Biblical Basis of Christian Spirituality.* Philadelphia: Westminster Press, 1960. A seminal study of the theme by one of the foremost interpreters of imitative spirituality.

Van Engen, John, ed. *Devotio Moderna: Basic Writings.* New York: Paulist Press, 1988. An extremely helpful anthology of the principle writings of this late medieval movement.

Comparison of Editions ☐

BOOK II

The Interior Life	Book II.	Book II.
1. Meditation	1.	1.
2. Humility	2.	2.
3. Goodness and Peace in Man	3.	3.
4. Purity of Mind and Unity of Purpose	4.	4.
5. Ourselves	5.	5.
6. The Joy of a Good Conscience	6.	6.
7. Loving Jesus Above All Things	7.	7.
8. The Intimate Friendship of Jesus	8.	8.
9. Wanting No Share in Comfort	9.	9.
10. Appreciating God's Grace	10.	10.
11. Few Love the Cross of Jesus	11.	11.
12. The Royal Road of the Holy Cross	12.	12.

BOOK III

Internal Consolation	Book III.	Book III.
1. The Inward Conversation of Christ with the Faithful Soul	1.	1.
2. Truth Speaks Inwardly Without the Sound of Words	2.	2.
3. Listen Humbly to the Words of God	3.	3.
4. We Must Walk Before God in Humility and Truth	4.	4.
5. The Wonderful Effect of Divine Love	5.	5.
6. The Proving of a True Lover	6.	Omitted
7. Grace Must Be Hidden Under the Mantle of Humility	7.	Omitted
8. Self-Abasement in the Sight of God	7.	6.
9. All Things Should be Referred to God as their Last End	8.	Omitted
10. To Despise the World and Serve God Is Sweet	9.	7.
11. The Longings of our Hearts Must Be Examined	10.	Omitted
12. Acquiring Patience in the Fight Against Concupiscence	Omitted	Omitted
13. The Obedience of One Humbly Subject to Jesus Christ	Omitted	Omitted
14. Consider the Hidden Judgments of God	11.	Omitted
15. How One Should Feel and Speak on Every Desirable Thing	12.	8.
16. True Comfort Is to Be Sought in God Alone	13.	Omitted
17. All Our Care Is to Be Placed in God	14.	9.
18. Temporal Sufferings Should Be Borne Patiently	Omitted	Omitted
19. True Patience in Suffering	15.	Omitted
20. Confessing Our Weakness in the Miseries of Life	Omitted	Omitted
21. Above All Goods and All Gifts We Must Rest in God	16.	10.
22. Remember the Innumerable Gifts of God	17.	Omitted

BOOK IV

An Invitation to Holy Communion	Book IV.	Book IV.
1. The Great Reverence with Which We Should Receive Christ	1.	1.
2. God's Great Goodness and Love	2.	2.
3. It Is Profitable to Receive Communion Often	3.	3.
4. Many Blessings Are Given Those Who Receive	4.	4.
5. The Dignity of the Sacrament and of the Priesthood	5.	5.
6. An Inquiry on the Proper Thing to Do Before Communion	Omitted	Omitted
7. The Examination of Conscience and the Resolution to Amend	6.	6.
8. The Offering of Christ on the Cross; Our Offering	7.	7.
9. We Should Offer Ourselves and All That We Have to God	8.	8.
10. Do Not Lightly Forego Holy Communion	Omitted	Omitted
11. The Body of Christ and Sacred Scripture	9.	9.
12. The Communicant Should Prepare Himself for Christ	10.	10.
13. With All Her Heart the Devout Soul Should Desire Union	10 & 11	10 & 11
14. The Ardent Longing of Devout Men for the Body of Christ	12.	12.
15. The Grace of Devotion Is Acquired Through Humility	13.	13.
16. We Should Show Our Needs to Christ and Ask His Grace	14.	14.
17. The Burning Love and Strong Desire to Receive Christ	15.	15.
18. Man Should Not Scrutinize This Sacrament in Curiosity	Omitted	Omitted

Scripture Index □

Christian Scriptures

Inspiration

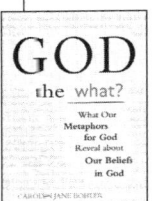

Finding Time for the Timeless: Spirituality in the Workweek
By John McQuiston II
Offers refreshing stories of everyday spiritual practices people use to free themselves from the work and worry mindset of our culture.
5⅛ x 6½, 208 pp, Quality PB, 978-1-59473-383-3 **$9.99**

God the What?: What Our Metaphors for God Reveal about Our Beliefs in God *by Carolyn Jane Bohler*
Inspires you to consider a wide range of images of God in order to refine how you imagine God. 6 x 9, 192 pp, Quality PB, 978-1-59473-251-5 **$16.99**

How Did I Get to Be 70 When I'm 35 Inside?: Spiritual Surprises of Later Life *by Linda Douty*
Encourages you to focus on the inner changes of aging to help you greet your later years as the grand adventure they can be. 6 x 9, 208 pp, Quality PB, 978-1-59473-297-3 **$16.99**

Restoring Life's Missing Pieces: The Spiritual Power of Remembering & Reuniting with People, Places, Things & Self *by Caren Goldman*
A powerful and thought-provoking look at reunions of all kinds as roads to remembering and re-membering ourselves.
6 x 9, 208 pp, Quality PB, 978-1-59473-295-9 **$16.99**

Saving Civility: 52 Ways to Tame Rude, Crude & Attitude for a Polite Planet
By Sara Hacala
Provides fifty-two practical ways you can reverse the course of incivility and make the world a more enriching, pleasant place to live.
6 x 9, 240 pp, Quality PB 978-1-59473-314-7 **$16.99**

Spiritually Healthy Divorce: Navigating Disruption with Insight & Hope
by Carolyne Call
A spiritual map to help you move through the twists and turns of divorce.
6 x 9, 224 pp, Quality PB, 978-1-59473-288-1 **$16.99**

Who Is My God? 2nd Edition
An Innovative Guide to Finding Your Spiritual Identity
by the Editors at SkyLight Paths
Provides the Spiritual Identity Self-Test™ to uncover the components of your unique spirituality. 6 x 9, 160 pp, Quality PB, 978-1-59473-014-6 **$15.99**

Journeys of Simplicity
Traveling Light with Thomas Merton, Bashō,
Edward Abbey, Annie Dillard & Others
by Philip Harnden
Invites you to consider a more graceful way of traveling through life.
PB includes journal pages to help you get started on
your own spiritual journey.
5 x 7¼, 144 pp, Quality PB, 978-1-59473-181-5 **$12.99**
5 x 7¼, 128 pp, HC, 978-1-893361-76-8 **$16.95**

Or phone, fax, mail or e-mail to: SKYLIGHT PATHS Publishing
Sunset Farm Offices, Route 4 • P.O. Box 237 • Woodstock, Vermont 05091
Tel: (802) 457-4000 • Fax: (802) 457-4004 • www.skylightpaths.com
Credit card orders: (800) 962-4544 (8:30AM–5:30PM EST Monday–Friday)
Generous discounts on quantity orders. SATISFACTION GUARANTEED. Prices subject to change.

Sacred Texts—SkyLight Illuminations Series

Offers today's spiritual seeker an enjoyable entry into the great classic texts of the world's spiritual traditions. Each classic is presented in an accessible translation, with facing pages of guided commentary from experts, giving you the keys you need to understand the history, context and meaning of the text.

CHRISTIANITY

Celtic Christian Spirituality: Essential Writings—Annotated & Explained
Annotation by Mary C. Earle; Foreword by John Philip Newell
Explores how the writings of this lively tradition embody the gospel.
5½ x 8½, 176 pp, Quality PB, 978-1-59473-302-4 **$16.99**

Desert Fathers and Mothers: Early Christian Wisdom Sayings—
Annotated & Explained
Annotation by Christine Valters Paintner, PhD
Opens up wisdom of the desert fathers and mothers for readers with no previous knowledge of Western monasticism and early Christianity.
5½ x 8½, 192 pp, Quality PB, 978-1-59473-373-4 **$16.99**

The End of Days: Essential Selections from Apocalyptic Texts—
Annotated & Explained
Annotation by Robert G. Clouse, PhD
Helps you understand the complex Christian visions of the end of the world.
5½ x 8½, 224 pp, Quality PB, 978-1-59473-170-9 **$16.99**

The Hidden Gospel of Matthew: Annotated & Explained
Translation & Annotation by Ron Miller
Discover the words and events that have the strongest connection to the historical Jesus.
5½ x 8½, 272 pp, Quality PB, 978-1-59473-038-2 **$16.99**

The Infancy Gospels of Jesus: Apocryphal Tales from the Childhoods of Mary and Jesus—Annotated & Explained
Translation & Annotation by Stevan Davies; Foreword by A. Edward Siecienski, PhD
A startling presentation of the early lives of Mary, Jesus and other biblical figures that will amuse and surprise you.
5½ x 8½, 176 pp, Quality PB, 978-1-59473-258-4 **$16.99**

John & Charles Wesley: Selections from Their Writings and Hymns—
Annotated & Explained
Annotation by Paul W. Chilcote, PhD
A unique presentation of the writings of these two inspiring brothers brings together some of the most essential material from their large corpus of work.
5½ x 8½, 288 pp, Quality PB, 978-1-59473-309-3 **$16.99**

The Lost Sayings of Jesus: Teachings from Ancient Christian, Jewish, Gnostic and Islamic Sources—Annotated & Explained
Translation & Annotation by Andrew Phillip Smith; Foreword by Stephan A. Hoeller
This collection of more than three hundred sayings depicts Jesus as a Wisdom teacher who speaks to people of all faiths as a mystic and spiritual master.
5½ x 8½, 240 pp, Quality PB, 978-1-59473-172-3 **$16.99**

Philokalia: The Eastern Christian Spiritual Texts—Selections
Annotated & Explained *Annotation by Allyne Smith; Translation by G. E. H. Palmer,*
Phillip Sherrard and Bishop Kallistos Ware
The first approachable introduction to the wisdom of the Philokalia, the classic text of Eastern Christian spirituality.
5½ x 8½, 240 pp, Quality PB, 978-1-59473-103-7 **$16.99**

The Sacred Writings of Paul: Selections Annotated & Explained
Translation & Annotation by Ron Miller
Leads you into the exciting immediacy of Paul's teachings.
5½ x 8½, 224 pp, Quality PB, 978-1-59473-213-3 **$16.99**

Sacred Texts—continued

CHRISTIANITY—continued

Saint Augustine of Hippo: Selections from *Confessions* and Other Essential Writings—Annotated & Explained
Annotation by Joseph T. Kelley, PhD; Translation by the Augustinian Heritage Institute
Provides insight into the mind and heart of this foundational Christian figure.
5½ x 8½, 272 pp, Quality PB, 978-1-59473-282-9 **$16.99**

Saint Ignatius Loyola—The Spiritual Writings: Selections
Annotated & Explained *Annotation by Mark Mossa, SJ*
Draws from contemporary translations of original texts focusing on the practical mysticism of Ignatius of Loyola.
5½ x 8½, 288 pp, Quality PB, 978-1-59473-301-7 **$16.99**

Sex Texts from the Bible: Selections Annotated & Explained
Translation & Annotation by Teresa J. Hornsby; Foreword by Amy-Jill Levine
Demystifies the Bible's ideas on gender roles, marriage, sexual orientation, virginity, lust and sexual pleasure.
5½ x 8½, 208 pp, Quality PB, 978-1-59473-217-1 **$16.99**

Spiritual Writings on Mary: Annotated & Explained
Annotation by Mary Ford-Grabowsky; Foreword by Andrew Harvey
Examines the role of Mary, the mother of Jesus, as a source of inspiration in history and in life today.
5½ x 8½, 288 pp, Quality PB, 978-1-59473-001-6 **$16.99**

The Way of a Pilgrim: The Jesus Prayer Journey—Annotated & Explained
Translation & Annotation by Gleb Pokrovsky; Foreword by Andrew Harvey
A classic of Russian Orthodox spirituality.
5½ x 8½, 160 pp, Illus., Quality PB, 978-1-893361-31-7 **$14.95**

Bible Stories / Folktales

Abraham's Bind & Other Bible Tales of Trickery, Folly, Mercy and Love by *Michael J. Caduto*
New retellings of episodes in the lives of familiar biblical characters explore relevant life lessons. 6 x 9, 224 pp, HC, 978-1-59473-186-0 **$19.99**

Daughters of the Desert: Stories of Remarkable Women from Christian, Jewish and Muslim Traditions by *Claire Rudolf Murphy,*
Meghan Nuttall Sayres, Mary Cronk Farrell, Sarah Conover and Betsy Wharton
Breathes new life into the old tales of our female ancestors in faith. Uses traditional scriptural passages as starting points, then with vivid detail fills in historical context and place. Chapters reveal the voices of Sarah, Hagar, Huldah, Esther, Salome, Mary Magdalene, Lydia, Khadija, Fatima and many more. Historical fiction ideal for readers of all ages.
5½ x 8½, 192 pp, Quality PB, 978-1-59473-106-8 **$14.99** Inc. reader's discussion guide
HC, 978-1-893361-72-0 **$19.95**

The Triumph of Eve & Other Subversive Bible Tales
by *Matt Biers-Ariel*
These engaging retellings of familiar Bible stories are witty, often hilarious and always profound. They invite you to grapple with questions and issues that are often hidden in the original texts.
5½ x 8½, 192 pp, Quality PB, 978-1-59473-176-1 **$14.99**

Also available: **The Triumph of Eve Teacher's Guide**
8½ x 11, 44 pp, PB, 978-1-59473-152-5 **$8.99**

Wisdom in the Telling
Finding Inspiration and Grace in Traditional Folktales and Myths Retold
by *Lorraine Hartin-Gelardi*
6 x 9, 192 pp, HC, 978-1-59473-185-3 **$19.99**

Spirituality

Gathering at God's Table: The Meaning of Mission in the Feast of Faith
By Katharine Jefferts Schori
A profound reminder of our role in the larger frame of God's dream for a restored and reconciled world.   6 x 9, 256 pp, HC, 978-1-59473-316-1 **$21.99**

The Heartbeat of God: Finding the Sacred in the Middle of Everything
by Katharine Jefferts Schori; Foreword by Joan Chittister, OSB
Explores our connections to other people, to other nations and with the environment through the lens of faith. 6 x 9, 240 pp, HC, 978-1-59473-292-8 **$21.99**

A Dangerous Dozen: Twelve Christians Who Threatened the Status Quo but Taught Us to Live Like Jesus
by the Rev. Canon C. K. Robertson, PhD; Foreword by Archbishop Desmond Tutu
Profiles twelve visionary men and women who challenged society and showed the world a different way of living. 6 x 9, 208 pp, Quality PB, 978-1-59473-298-0 **$16.99**

Decision Making & Spiritual Discernment: The Sacred Art of Finding Your Way *by Nancy L. Bieber*
Presents three essential aspects of Spirit-led decision making: willingness, attentiveness and responsiveness. 5½ x 8½, 208 pp, Quality PB, 978-1-59473-289-8 **$16.99**

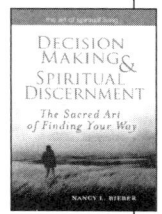

Laugh Your Way to Grace: Reclaiming the Spiritual Power of Humor
by Rev. Susan Sparks   A powerful, humorous case for laughter as a spiritual, healing path.   6 x 9, 176 pp, Quality PB, 978-1-59473-280-5 **$16.99**

Bread, Body, Spirit: Finding the Sacred in Food
Edited and with Introductions by Alice Peck   6 x 9, 224 pp, Quality PB, 978-1-59473-242-3 **$19.99**

Claiming Earth as Common Ground: The Ecological Crisis through the Lens of Faith
by Andrea Cohen-Kiener; Foreword by Rev. Sally Bingham
6 x 9, 192 pp, Quality PB, 978-1-59473-261-4 **$16.99**

Creating a Spiritual Retirement: A Guide to the Unseen Possibilities in Our Lives
by Molly Srode   6 x 9, 208 pp, b/w photos, Quality PB, 978-1-59473-050-4 **$14.99**

Creative Aging: Rethinking Retirement and Non-Retirement in a Changing World
by Marjory Zoet Bankson   6 x 9, 160 pp, Quality PB, 978-1-59473-281-2 **$16.99**

Keeping Spiritual Balance as We Grow Older: More than 65 Creative Ways to Use Purpose, Prayer, and the Power of Spirit to Build a Meaningful Retirement
by Molly and Bernie Srode   8 x 8, 224 pp, Quality PB, 978-1-59473-042-9 **$16.99**

Hearing the Call across Traditions: Readings on Faith and Service
Edited by Adam Davis; Foreword by Eboo Patel
6 x 9, 352 pp, Quality PB, 978-1-59473-303-1 **$18.99**; HC, 978-1-59473-264-5 **$29.99**

Honoring Motherhood: Prayers, Ceremonies & Blessings
Edited and with Introductions by Lynn L. Caruso
5 x 7¼, 272 pp, Quality PB, 978-1-58473-384-0 **$9.99**; HC, 978-1-59473-239-3 **$19.99**

The Losses of Our Lives: The Sacred Gifts of Renewal in Everyday Loss
by Dr. Nancy Copeland-Payton   6 x 9, 192 pp, HC, 978-1-59473-271-3 **$19.99**

Renewal in the Wilderness: A Spiritual Guide to Connecting with God in the Natural World *by John Lionberger*
6 x 9, 176 pp, b/w photos, Quality PB, 978-1-59473-219-5 **$16.99**

Soul Fire: Accessing Your Creativity
by Thomas Ryan, CSP   6 x 9, 160 pp, Quality PB, 978-1-59473-243-0 **$16.99**

A Spirituality for Brokenness: Discovering Your Deepest Self in Difficult Times
by Terry Taylor   6 x 9, 176 pp, Quality PB, 978-1-59473-229-4 **$16.99**

A Walk with Four Spiritual Guides: Krishna, Buddha, Jesus, and Ramakrishna
by Andrew Harvey   5½ x 8½, 192 pp, b/w photos & illus., Quality PB, 978-1-59473-138-9 **$15.99**

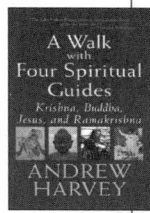

The Workplace and Spirituality: New Perspectives on Research and Practice
Edited by Dr. Joan Marques, Dr. Satinder Dhiman and Dr. Richard King
6 x 9, 256 pp, HC, 978-1-59473-260-7 **$29.99**

Spiritual Practice

Fly-Fishing—The Sacred Art: Casting a Fly as a Spiritual Practice
by Rabbi Eric Eisenkramer and Rev. Michael Attas, MD; Foreword by Chris Wood, CEO,
Trout Unlimited; Preface by Lori Simon, executive director, Casting for Recovery
Shares what fly-fishing can teach you about reflection, awe and wonder; the benefits of solitude; the blessing of community and the search for the Divine.
5½ x 8½, 160 pp, Quality PB, 978-1-59473-299-7 **$16.99**

Lectio Divina—The Sacred Art: Transforming Words & Images into
Heart-Centered Prayer *by Christine Valters Paintner, PhD*
Expands the practice of sacred reading beyond scriptural texts and makes it
accessible in contemporary life. 5½ x 8½, 240 pp, Quality PB, 978-1-59473-300-0 **$16.99**

Writing—The Sacred Art: Beyond the Page to Spiritual Practice
By Rami Shapiro and Aaron Shapiro
Push your writing through the trite and the boring to something fresh, something
transformative. Includes over fifty unique, practical exercises.
5½ x 8½, 192 pp, Quality PB, 978-1-59473-372-7 **$16.99**

Dance—The Sacred Art: The Joy of Movement as a Spiritual Practice
by Cynthia Winton-Henry 5½ x 8½, 224 pp, Quality PB, 978-1-59473-268-3 **$16.99**

Everyday Herbs in Spiritual Life: A Guide to Many Practices
by Michael J. Caduto; Foreword by Rosemary Gladstar
7 x 9, 208 pp, 20+ b/w illus., Quality PB, 978-1-59473-174-7 **$16.99**

Giving—The Sacred Art: Creating a Lifestyle of Generosity
by Lauren Tyler Wright 5½ x 8½, 208 pp, Quality PB, 978-1-59473-224-9 **$16.99**

Haiku—The Sacred Art: A Spiritual Practice in Three Lines
by Margaret D. McGee 5½ x 8½, 192 pp, Quality PB, 978-1-59473-269-0 **$16.99**

Hospitality—The Sacred Art: Discovering the Hidden Spiritual Power of Invitation
and Welcome *by Rev. Nanette Sawyer; Foreword by Rev. Dirk Ficca*
5½ x 8½, 208 pp, Quality PB, 978-1-59473-228-7 **$16.99**

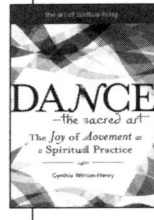

Labyrinths from the Outside In: Walking to Spiritual Insight—A Beginner's Guide
by Donna Schaper and Carole Ann Camp
6 x 9, 208 pp, b/w illus. and photos, Quality PB, 978-1-893361-18-8 **$16.95**

Practicing the Sacred Art of Listening: A Guide to Enrich Your Relationships
and Kindle Your Spiritual Life *by Kay Lindahl* 8 x 8, 176 pp, Quality PB, 978-1-893361-85-0 **$16.95**

Recovery—The Sacred Art: The Twelve Steps as Spiritual Practice *by Rami Shapiro;*
Foreword by Joan Borysenko, PhD 5½ x 8½, 240 pp, Quality PB, 978-1-59473-259-1 **$16.99**

Running—The Sacred Art: Preparing to Practice *by Dr. Warren A. Kay; Foreword by*
Kristin Armstrong 5½ x 8½, 160 pp, Quality PB, 978-1-59473-227-0 **$16.99**

The Sacred Art of Chant: Preparing to Practice
by Ana Hernández 5½ x 8½, 192 pp, Quality PB, 978-1-59473-036-8 **$15.99**

The Sacred Art of Fasting: Preparing to Practice
by Thomas Ryan, CSP 5½ x 8½, 192 pp, Quality PB, 978-1-59473-078-8 **$15.99**

The Sacred Art of Forgiveness: Forgiving Ourselves and Others through God's Grace
by Marcia Ford 8 x 8, 176 pp, Quality PB, 978-1-59473-175-4 **$18.99**

The Sacred Art of Listening: Forty Reflections for Cultivating a Spiritual Practice
by Kay Lindahl; Illus. by Amy Schnapper 8 x 8, 160 pp, b/w illus., Quality PB, 978-1-893361-44-7 **$16.99**

The Sacred Art of Lovingkindness: Preparing to Practice
by Rabbi Rami Shapiro; Foreword by Marcia Ford 5½ x 8½, 176 pp, Quality PB, 978-1-59473-151-8 **$16.99**

Sacred Attention: A Spiritual Practice for Finding God in the Moment
by Margaret D. McGee 6 x 9, 144 pp, Quality PB, 978-1-59473-291-1 **$16.99**

Soul Fire: Accessing Your Creativity
by Thomas Ryan, CSP 6 x 9, 160 pp, Quality PB, 978-1-59473-243-0 **$16.99**

Spiritual Adventures in the Snow: Skiing & Snowboarding as Renewal for Your Soul
by Dr. Marcia McFee and Rev. Karen Foster; Foreword by Paul Arthur
5½ x 8½, 208 pp, Quality PB, 978-1-59473-270-6 **$16.99**

Thanking & Blessing—The Sacred Art: Spiritual Vitality through Gratefulness
by Jay Marshall, PhD; Foreword by Philip Gulley 5½ x 8½, 176 pp, Quality PB, 978-1-59473-231-7 **$16.99**

Prayer / Meditation

Men Pray: Voices of Strength, Faith, Healing, Hope and Courage
Created by the Editors at SkyLight Paths
Celebrates the rich variety of ways men around the world have called out to the Divine—with words of joy, praise, gratitude, wonder, petition and even anger—from the ancient world up to our own day.
5 x 7, 200 pp (est), HC, 978-1-59473-395-6 **$16.99**

Sacred Attention: A Spiritual Practice for Finding God in the Moment
by Margaret D. McGee
Framed on the Christian liturgical year, this inspiring guide explores ways to develop a practice of attention as a means of talking—and listening—to God.
6 x 9, 144 pp, Quality PB, 978-1-59473-291-1 **$16.99**

Women of Color Pray: Voices of Strength, Faith, Healing, Hope and Courage
Edited and with Introductions by Christal M. Jackson
Through these prayers, poetry, lyrics, meditations and affirmations, you will share in the strong and undeniable connection women of color share with God.
5 x 7¼, 208 pp, Quality PB, 978-1-59473-077-1 **$15.99**

The Art of Public Prayer, 2nd Edition: Not for Clergy Only
by Lawrence A. Hoffman, PhD 6 x 9, 288 pp, Quality PB, 978-1-893361-06-5 **$19.99**

A Heart of Stillness: A Complete Guide to Learning the Art of Meditation
by David A. Cooper 5½ x 8½, 272 pp, Quality PB, 978-1-893361-03-4 **$18.99**

Living into Hope: A Call to Spiritual Action for Such a Time as This
by Rev. Dr. Joan Brown Campbell; Foreword by Karen Armstrong
6 x 9, 208 pp, HC, 978-1-59473-283-6 **$21.99**

Meditation without Gurus: A Guide to the Heart of Practice
by Clark Strand 5½ x 8½, 192 pp, Quality PB, 978-1-893361-93-5 **$16.95**

Prayers to an Evolutionary God
by William Cleary; Afterword by Diarmuid O'Murchu
6 x 9, 208 pp, HC, 978-1-59473-006-1 **$21.99**

Praying with Our Hands: 21 Practices of Embodied Prayer from the World's
Spiritual Traditions *by Jon M. Sweeney; Photos by Jennifer J. Wilson; Foreword by Mother Tessa Bielecki; Afterword by Taitetsu Unno, PhD*
8 x 8, 96 pp, 22 duotone photos, Quality PB, 978-1-893361-16-4 **$16.95**

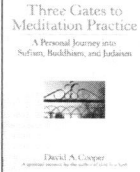

Secrets of Prayer: A Multifaith Guide to Creating Personal Prayer in Your Life
by Nancy Corcoran, CSJ
6 x 9, 160 pp, Quality PB, 978-1-59473-215-7 **$16.99**

Three Gates to Meditation Practice: A Personal Journey into Sufism, Buddhism,
and Judaism *by David A. Cooper* 5½ x 8½, 240 pp, Quality PB, 978-1-893361-22-5 **$16.95**

Prayer / M. Basil Pennington, OCSO

Finding Grace at the Center, 3rd Edition: The Beginning of
Centering Prayer *with Thomas Keating, OCSO, and Thomas E. Clarke, SJ; Foreword by Rev. Cynthia Bourgeault, PhD* A practical guide to a simple and beautiful form of meditative prayer. 5 x 7¼, 128 pp, Quality PB, 978-1-59473-182-2 **$12.99**

The Monks of Mount Athos: A Western Monk's Extraordinary
Spiritual Journey on Eastern Holy Ground *Foreword by Archimandrite Dionysios*
Explores the landscape, monastic communities and food of Athos.
6 x 9, 352 pp, Quality PB, 978-1-893361-78-2 **$18.95**

Psalms: A Spiritual Commentary *Illus. by Phillip Ratner*
Reflections on some of the most beloved passages from the Bible's most widely read book. 6 x 9, 176 pp, 24 full-page b/w illus., Quality PB, 978-1-59473-234-8 **$16.99**

The Song of Songs: A Spiritual Commentary *Illus. by Phillip Ratner*
Explore the Bible's most challenging mystical text.
6 x 9, 160 pp, 14 full-page b/w illus., Quality PB, 978-1-59473-235-5 **$16.99**
HC, 978-1-59473-004-7 **$19.99**

About SKYLIGHT PATHS Publishing

SkyLight Paths Publishing is creating a place where people of different spiritual traditions come together for challenge and inspiration, a place where we can help each other understand the mystery that lies at the heart of our existence.

Through spirituality, our religious beliefs are increasingly becoming a part of our lives—rather than *apart* from our lives. While many of us may be more interested than ever in spiritual growth, we may be less firmly planted in traditional religion. Yet, we do want to deepen our relationship to the sacred, to learn from our own as well as from other faith traditions, and to practice in new ways.

SkyLight Paths sees both believers and seekers as a community that increasingly transcends traditional boundaries of religion and denomination—people wanting to learn from each other, *walking together, finding the way.*

For your information and convenience, at the back of this book we have provided a list of other SkyLight Paths books you might find interesting and useful. They cover the following subjects:

Buddhism / Zen	Global Spiritual	Monasticism
Catholicism	Perspectives	Mysticism
Children's Books	Gnosticism	Poetry
Christianity	Hinduism /	Prayer
Comparative	Vedanta	Religious Etiquette
Religion	Inspiration	Retirement
Current Events	Islam / Sufism	Spiritual Biography
Earth-Based	Judaism	Spiritual Direction
Spirituality	Kabbalah	Spirituality
Enneagram	Meditation	Women's Interest
	Midrash Fiction	Worship

Or phone, fax, mail or e-mail to: SKYLIGHT PATHS Publishing
Sunset Farm Offices, Route 4 • P.O. Box 237 • Woodstock, Vermont 05091
Tel: (802) 457-4000 • Fax: (802) 457-4004 • www.skylightpaths.com
Credit card orders: (800) 962-4544 (8:30AM–5:30PM EST Monday–Friday)
Generous discounts on quantity orders. SATISFACTION GUARANTEED. Prices subject to change.

For more information about each book, visit our website at www.skylightpaths.com